THEORY AND PRINCIPLES OF EDUCATION

Edited by
Dr. A R. Rather
Department of Education
Kashmir University
Srinagar

D P H

DISCOVERY PUBLISHING HOUSE
NEW DELHI-110002

First Published – 2004

Reprinted – 2023

ISBN: 978-81-7141-817-6

Theory and Principles of Education

Published by:

DISCOVERY PUBLISHING HOUSE

4383/4B, Ansari Road, Darya Ganj

New Delhi-110 002 (India)

Phone: +91-11-23279245; 23253475; 43596065

+91 9811179893 / +91 9871656464

E-mail: discoverybooksindia@gmail.com

orderdphbooks@gmail.com

namitwasan9@gmail.com

web: www.discoverypublishinggroup.com

Printed at:

Infinity Imaging Systems

Delhi

Contents

Preface

Teachers' Training is a vital part of Education. Therefore, all efforts of the educationists, educators and instructors are aimed at the task of providing better training to the 'would be teachers' for their better education and proper growth, as a benefactor. No doubt, this responsibility can only be exercised, if the educators are equipped with the required knowledge of the subject concerned and the trainees develop needed interest in it. That's why, it becomes essential for making adequate provisions for each course to the teachers and as well as trainees. This series is designed for providing a solid practical base for all the papers. The series has been prepared strictly according to the B.Ed. syllabus, prescribed by universities.

Of course there are many a book on the subject, presently available in the market. But every author has his or her own style and way of presentation. The present work also has its own features, characteristics and significance. While preparing this series of books, the editor had to refer to the works of other authors and various sources for information. He expresses a deep gratitude for incorporating their ideas in the text. Hopefully, this series would serve as perfect reference material for all teachers, teacher-students and other readers also. If that much is achieved, the undersigned would feel contented and honoured.

–Editor

Syllabus

THEORY & PRINCIPLES OF EDUCATION

Unit I. Education & Philosophy

(i) Nature & Meaning of Education

(ii) Aims of Education – Individual and Social.

(iii) Nature and Meaning of Philosophy

(iv) Relation between Philosophy & Education

(v) Significance of Philosophy of Education

Unit II. Major Philosophies of Education

(i) Naturalism

(ii) Idealism

(iii) Pragmatism

(iv) Existentialism

These Educational Philosophies shall be discussed with special reference to Aims, Curriculum, Role of Teacher & Concept of Discipline.

Unit III. Educational Thinkers & their Contribution in Developing Principles of Education

(i) M.K. Gandhi : Basic Education

(ii) Tagore : Shanti Niketan

(iii) Swami Vivekananda : Man-making Education

(iv) John Dewey : Learning by Doing

(v) Froebel : The play-way Method

(vi) Montessori : The Didactic Apparatus

1

Meaning, Nature and Scope of Education

Education is never ending. It starts with the birth of an individual and then it goes on till the last day of the individual. Education makes an individual a real human being. It is an essential human virtue. Man becomes man through education. He learns something at every moment and on every day. Education equips the individual with social, moral, cultural and spiritual aspects and thus makes life progressive, cultured and civilized. About education, P.O. Bannerji said, "It is the development of the power of adaptation to an ever changing social environment."

Gone are the days when education was the right of a privileged few. Now all have the equal right to be educated as education has become *sine quo non* of civilisation.

Etymological Meaning of 'Education'

Let us understand the word 'Education' etymologically :

First view is that the word 'education' is derived from the latin word 'Educatum' which means 'to bring up' or 'to nourish'.

Second view is that the word 'education' is derived from the latin word 'education' which means 'to find out', or 'to draw out'. Naturally here in the process of education, 'effort is to draw out' rather than 'to put in'.

Third view is that the word education comes from the Latin word 'Education' which means the 'act of teaching or training'.

Concept of Education: Indian Views

1. According to Rig Veda, "Education is something which makes a man self-reliant and selfless.
2. According to Upanishads, "Education is that whose end product is salvation".
3. The well known Indian Economist Kautilya says, "Education means training for the country and for the nation.
4. The Indian Philosopher Shankaracharya considers education as "the realisation of the self."
5. Swami Vivekanand considered education as "the manifestation of divine perfection of existing in man."
6. According to Vedantic view point. The essence of man is spirituality. We need an education that quickens, that kindles the urge of spirituality inherent in every mind."
7. According to Mahatma Gandhi, "By education I mean an all round drawing out of the best in child and man-body, mind and spirit."
8. Guru Nanak said, "Education is self-realization and service of the people."
9. Aurobindo Ghosh puts forth his view on education as. "Helping the growing soul to draw out that is in itself".
10. Rabindra Nath Tagore says, "Education means enabling the mind to find out that ultimate truth which emancipates us from the bondage of the dust and gives us the wealth, not of things but of inner light, not of power but of love, making this truth its own and gives expression to ."

11. In the words of Zakir Hussain, "Education is the process of the individual mind" getting to its full possible development. It is a long school which lasts a life-time."
12. According to Swami Dayanand, "Education is a means for character formation and righteous living."
13. In the words of University Education Commission Report (1948-49): "Education to the Indian traditions, is not merely a means of earning a living; nor it is only a nursery of thought or a school for citizenship. It is initiation into the life of spirit, a training of human soul in the pursuit of truth and the practice of virtue. It is a second birth, divitiyam janma."
14. According to the Report of Indian Education Commission (1964-66), "Education ought to be related to the life, needs and aspirations of the people and thereby made powerful instrument of social, economic and cultural transformation."

The Concept : Western View

Concept of education as given by a few popular Western thinkers is as given below:-

1. Plato's view: "Education is the capacity to feel pleasure and pain at the right moment. It develops in the body and in the soul of the pupil all the beauty and all the perfection of which he is capable of."
2. According to Aristotle, "Education is the creation of a sound mind in a sound body....It develops man's faculty, especially his mind, so that he may be able tb enjoy the contemplation of supreme truth, goodness and beauty in which perfect happiness essentially consists."
3. Socrates said, "Education means the bringing out of the ideas of universal validity which are latent in the mind of every man."
4. In the words of Comenfus, "All who are born as human beings, need education because they are destined to be

real men, not wild beasts, dull animals and clumps of wood."

5. Thompson said, "Education is the influence of environment on the individual with the view to producing a permanent change in his habits of behaviour, of thought and of attitude."

6. Pestalozzi remarked, "Education is natural, harmonious and progressive development of man's innate powers."

7. Adams said, "Education is a conscious and deliberate process by which one personality acts upon another in order to modify the development of the other by the communication and manipulation of knowledge."

8. Froebel's view, "Education is the unfoldment of what is already enfolded in the germ. It is the process through which the child makes internal external."

9. In the words of Milton, "I call, therefore a complete and generous education that which fits a man to perform justly, skillfully and maghanimously all the offices, both private and public, of peace and war."

10. According to T.P. Nunn, "Education is the complete development of individuality so-that he makes an original contribution to human life according to the best of his capacity."

11. John Dewey says, "Education is the process of living through a continuous reconstruction of experiences. It is the development of those capacities in the individual which will enable him to control his environment and fulfil his possibilities."

12. Herbert's view, "Education is the development of good character."

13. In the words of Redden, "Education is the deliberate and systematic influence, exerted by the mature person upon the immature, through instruction, discipline and harmonious development of physical, inteliectual,

aesthetic, social and spiritual powers of the human being, according to individual and social needs and directed 'towards the union of the educated with his creators as the final end."

14. Draver says, "Education is a process in which and by which knowledge, character and behaviour of the young are shaped and moulded."
15. According to Kant, "Education is the development in the individual of all the perfection of which he is capable."
16. According to Ross, " The aim of education is the development of valuable personality and spiritual individuality."

Narrower Concept

in a limited sense, education is confined to the school and the University instruction. Education starts from the day a child is admitted in a school and it ends when the child completes studies and leaves at the college or University stage. Here education is limited to class room teaching. It is formal in nature. The different examinations passed indicate his success of education. This type of education is intentional and not incidental. It is consciously received education and it is imparted by the institution through an organised way. The curriculum of studies is also of definite type. Here everything is pre-planned and education is given by the teachers in the class room controlled situations. Here education is synonymous with instruction.

Broader Concept

in the broader sense, education means the totality of experience gained by an individual from birth to death. It is not the communication of information by the teacher. It is also not just the acquisition of knowlege by the student. The fact is that it is the total development of the personality. Here learning is through any agency such as home, street, school, society, temple, play-ground, cinema etc. In this regard William H. Kilpatnck said, "From the broad point of view, all life heartfully lived is education." Here the curriculum 'for studies is unlimited and also indefinite. Mark Hopkins says, "Education in its widest sense includes everything that exerts a formative influence."

Edward Thring said, "Education is the transmission of life, by the living to the living." in short we can say that education is life and life is education.

T. Raymont remarked: One is educated by one's vocation, by home life, by friendship, by marriage, by parenthood, by reaction, by travel, and so forth."

According to the Report of international Commission on the development of education - "Learning to be' ......human beings keep on learning and training themselves throughout lives, above and through the influence of the surrounding environment and through the experiences which mould their behaviour, their conceptions of life and the content of their knowledge."

Narrow and broad meanings of education have to be reconciled. Surely they are complementary to each other. The following lines by the well known educationaists satisfy the whole thing:

According to Gibbons : "Every person has two educations : one which he receives from others and one more important, which he gives to himself."

Wbitehead said: "There is only one subject matter of education and that is life in all its manifestations."

The Nature

1. Education is a tri-polar process where teacher taught and social environment act and react with one antoher.
2. Education is a never ending venture.
3. It is a process where some purpose/purposes are aimed at and efforts accordingly are made to attain them.
4. It is a life-long process.
5. Education is preparation for We through Me experience.

6. It is a process of individual development.
7. It is dynamic.
8. It is rotated to time, place and social set up life.
9. It is both theoretical and practical.
10. It is science as well as art.
11. It is an instrument which is used to attain better life.
12. It is an essential human virtue because man becomes man through it.
13. Education is essentially a process of growth and development which goes on throughout life.
14. Education is the modification of behaviour.
15. Education is getting new knowledge and a new reactions.
16. Education is adjustment with the environment.

Instruction

Instruction is an integral part of education. The process of instruction generally goes on in the class room situations. Some knowledge is put into the mind of the child and he is expected to memorise it.

According to international Dictionary of Education: "instruction is often used synonymously with teaching but often specific teaching is akin to the skill of training rather than to education in a broader sense. It may be audio-visual, correspondence or individual."

It includes the activities dealing directly with the teaching of students. It is given for improving the quality of teaching.

The following are the characteristics of instruction:

1. Instruction is an integral part of education. It often goes on when a group of learners are there. It is not possible in the vacuum.

2. Instruction is not spontaneous. Rather it is pre-planned activity.
3. It helps in giving knowledge systematically.
4. Instructions are instructor oriented. The teacher is the giver and the child receives instruction passively.
5. The process of instruction goes on in a limited context only.
6. It is mostly examination oriented. The purpose of giving instruction is enabling the student to pass the examination.
7. The person who gives instruction does need language, proficiency.
8. Its main limitation is that it does not develop interest in the students. It also does not imbibe any values in the learners.

Training

Training is an integral part of education, we compare education with, a circle training is then a segment of circle, in training, practical activity is involved) Training helps an individual reach a set standard of behaviour. There is always a set programme to be followed. Thus in the air force, training is given to make the individual an expert pilot. Training is given for car driving, scooter driving etc. In all these cases, some instructor is always there to give training.

Thus training is a specific programme of vocational preparation. It is a planned and systematic sequence of instruction under competent supervisor. It may include refresher and reorientation training for professionals.

Training is a time bound process. After the expiry of certain period, we say that training is over. Then the person becomes a fit person in that field.

The following are the characteristics of training:

1. Training is given in a formal way. Some agency is always working behind it.

2. In training, there are rigid rules and regulations and those have to be observed carefully.
3. Training is given by expert person of the field.
4. It is a practical activity.
5. Framing may or may not make an individual socially efficient.
6. Through training, the expert tries to formulate a set type of behaviour of the individual. Arguments or reasoning of any type are not welcome here.
7. Training is a part of education. Education aims at all round development of an individual whereas training imparts some practical skill or skills.
8. It is a time bound process.

Indoctrination

Indoctrination is an activity which helps in forming beliefs. Some ideas are infused in the minds of the learners from the beginning. Those ideas are continuously put in the mind and thus ideas become their firm beliefs. Once the ideas or beliefs are fixed in the mind then time can't easily shake off those deep rooted ideas or beliefs from them.

Broadly, indoctrination is the attempt to inculcate or fix in the individual a certain pattern of beliefs or habits. It may occur in any teaching learning situation. More strictly, it is an attempt to insinuate into the experience of the individual any doctrine whether social, political, economic or religious.

People are indoctrinated to believe certain things. In the process of indoctrination, there is almost negligible scope for reasoning.

Education brings desirable changes in beliefs, attitudes, values etc. Naturally education is something bigger and indoctrination is a part of it.

The following characteristics of indoctrination show its nature:

1. Indoctrination shapes the beliefs and transmits knowledge.

2. There is no scope for reasoning.
3. It makes the individuals believe certain things. There may or may not be any rational thinking behind.
4. Indoctrination is a sort of strategy which may be used as per the desire of the doer or as per requirement of the situation.
5. It is a part of education.

In this fast changing arena of life, indoctrination can be used as a strategy and the results can be wonderful. To bring about desirable social change, indoctrination may be used to make the people believe certain things.

Various Types

Education is an organised and imparted can be classified as under:

1. Formal Education 2. Informal Education 3. Non-formal Education.

Formal Education

Formal education is that which is provided in a formal way by observing all types of formalities. It is a pre-planned type of education, where specific alms are well fixed in advance, methods of teaching are decided and knowledge is given to the selected pupils by the selected teachers. This type of education ts imparted in the schools, colleges and universities where the learners abide toy the rules and regulations of the agency of formal education. Formal type of education is also provided in the library. It is limited to a specified period.

It is a consciously received education for which deliberate efforts are made both by the teacher and the learner. This type of education is well-organised and so it may anywhere in the school or outside the school. There, is a well-defined and clear cut curriculum. It is not confined to the schools only. In short, we can say that any teaching where there is instruction, supervision, definite aims etc., is called formal education. No matter whether it is given in the school or at home.

Characteristics

1. It is a well-known type of education well-cared for, well-aspired for and well-advocated.
2. Many tyes of formalities are observed here.
3. There is set of curriculum. Effort is there to modernise it as far as possible.
4. There are fixed goals and conscious efforts are always on to achieve the goals.
5. It is an organised type of education. Its show off is made as good as possible. It is made public to attract more and more learners.
6. It is a well-planned activity with fixed time table specially prepared for It.
7. Both the teacher and the taught make conscious efforts in the process of teaching learning.
8. The place of education and the timings are fixed here.
9. This type of education has a beginning and also the close.
10. Surely the syllabi are completed.
11. Examinations are held in a formal way and results announced keeping in view the goals fixed up.

Advantages

1. A student is able to sit in the company of other students of the same age group. That increases peer relationships, fellow feelings for one another.
2. In the formal system, many students get the opportunity of being together in different classes for a good deal of time. They have better understanding with each other.
3. It makes the students learn things in a disciplined way.

That gradually imbibes the quality of self-discipline in the students.

4. Here education is a continuous process and naturally it develops in the learners the habit of reading continuously.
5. "Education is in accordance with the growth and development of the different faculties of the learners. Thus it helps in having well cared for growth and development of the learners.

Disadvantages

1. Good and bad students, gifted and backward are generally made to sit together in the same class and taught by the same teachers. This shows down the ongoing rapid progress of the gifted pupils.
2. Every student has to wait for the expiry of the academic session and then only he/she gets promotion of the next class.
3. A few students may be keen to cover up more syllabus in less time. That is obstructed here in Indian system of formal education.
4. There are strains on the minds of the learners.
5. It is more or less unnatural way of teaching learning. There is artificial situations created when teaching-learning is conducted.
6. There is need of motivating the students. Sometimes student may fail to learn anything inspite of motivation by the teachers.

Informal Education

Education for which no formalities are observed is known as informal type of education. In this type of education, there is modification of the behaviour of the learner but no conscious efforts are made for it. Whatever is learnt here is not preplanmed. It is rather incidental. Here neither the teacher nor the lean is conscious of the process of teaching learning. For example, a person goes to the playground for physical exercise and there comes across someone who tells him very good ways of utilizing leisure time. Surely in this situation one acted as a teacher and the listener was a student but none of them was conscious of the fact that the process of teaching learning occurred informally. In this way through our daily routine of life, teaching learning may take place and we are quite unaware of it. This type of education is known as informal education. It is a casual type of education which is received through daily experiences and activities.

In this type of education there are no pre-determined aims, no definite curriculum, no well thought methods of teaching, no qualified and trained teachers and no definite place of education. Here education is received by the company of friends, relatives, community etc. Whatever as education is received plays a very important and significant role in the life of the education. This type of education may result into learning something wrong or bad. That is negative education and that may create some problems.

Characteristics

1. This type of education is informal because no formalities are observed here.
2. No conscious efforts are made either by the teacher or the taught.
3. It is in no way pre-planned activity.
4. It is incidental.
5. No formal goals are fixed up.
6. No formal means are used to attain the goals.
7. There are no fixed/appointed teachers. Any and eveybody can be a teacher in an informal situation.
8. Here a situation might crop up where the student may teach a teacher something.

9. There is no prescribed curriculum and no time-table is observed.
10. There is none who organises this type of education. It is all a matter of chance that teaching in learning occurs.
11. There is no fixed place for it.
12. This type of education is never completed and there is no fixed syllabus.
13. There are no examinations of any type.
14. It is all a natural way of teaching-learning.

Advantages

1. There are no strains of any type on the mind of the learner.
2. It is a natural way of teaching learning.
3. The learner is self-motivated in the process of learning.
4. Most of the learnt things are situational as they are learnt in one situation or the other. So they are remembered for a long time.
5. In this type of education there is no dependence on rote learning.

Disadvantages

1. It does not give much confidence to tne learner. Inspite of good knowledge, the learner may feel inferiority complex in a group of highly educated persons.
2. Here education is received in the absence of a so called 'guru' - the teacher. One may not learn the right things.
3. Whatever is expected to be learnt in the company of equal age group, that is missed here. Class fellow feelings, discipline, good habits, attitude etc. may not be acquired properly and rightly.

A Comparison between Formal and Informal Types

The following points of comparison indicate clearly the difference between formal and informal types of educations:

Formal Education	*In-formal Education*
1. Here all type of formalities are are observed.	1. Here no formalities observed.
2. Goals are fixed in a formal way.	2. No goals are fixed.
3. Proper means are used to achieve the goals.	3. No proper means are used.
4. Conscious efforts are made both are by the teacher and the learner and in the process of teaching-learning.	4. No conscious efforts made by the teacher taught.
5. Apparently it is an artificial way of teaching-learning.	5. In appearance, it is a type of teaching-learning.
6. Anybody may acters teacher in a situation. Even a student may, some times, play the role of a teacher in some situation.	6. Only a qualified person can act as a as a teacher and his duty is to impart education.
7. There is prescribed syllabus here.	7. There is no prescribed syllabus always.
8. No time-table. Things happen out of chance or by mere coincidence as they say.	8. There is always a formal type fixed time-table in vogue during the process of teaching-learning.
9. Efforts are there to teach in accordance with the prescribed syllabus.	9. No specific efforts are ever applied in one specific direction or the other.
10. Syllabus is completed through the and formal type of education,	10. There is no syllabus so there is no question of completing the syllabus.

Formal Education	In-formal Education
11. It is always organised type of education. Some organised body is no is behind the establishment of hind or the school.	11. It is unorganised type will be education. There organised body in the background.
12. The schools at a fixed place.	12. There is no school and no place is fixed. Education may be given at any place.
13. Work schedule is fixed.	13. No work-schedule is for it.
14. Rules and regulations are there and obedience of those is mandatory, for all the learners of that school.	14. There are no rules regulations. So there is no questions of obedience of those rules and regulations.
15. Restricted type of freedom is to be given to the learners and the teacher.	15. All type of freedom is given to the teachers and the learner.
16. It is started at a particular age, for is continued and thus over the years it is completed. Start is not possible at all stages of age.	16. There is no age limit for the starting or completion of this type of education. It is ever going and never ending
17. Its result is always good eehicatioft because everything is pre-planned and the process of education goes on under supervision.	17. It may result into negative learning because the learner may acquire certain bad habits, wrong attitudes etc.

Non-formal Education

Non-formal education has become popular during the recent past. Non-formal education is in between the formal and informal types of education, It is midway, because it is partly formal and partly informal. It is both intentional and incidental. This type of education is imparted outside the format school system.' For providing this type of education, there are no' restrictions of any type learners of any age group in service anywhere or unemployed can seek admission and receive education. A few examples of this system of education are open school, open university, correspondence course etc.

The system of non-formal education is parallel to formal education.

The only difference is that in this system there is flexibility almost at every step i.e. In admission, mode of instruction, curriculum etc. There are rules and regulations but there is no rigidity. Here different media are used for educating the people. Surely this approach is education to the doors of the learners who could not or are unable to receive formal education due to any reason.

Some experts put forth their views on non-formal education:

1. According to Coombs'. "Non-formal education is one which is imparted through organisation and institutions, outside the formal education institutions."
2. Handerson's view. "Non-formal education is far wider and more inclusive than schooling, which imparts wider experiences out of school."
3. In the words of McCall's : "Non-formal education is the entire range of learning experiences outside of the regular graded school system."
4. According to Bremworks: "Non-formal education differs from formal education from the promixity to immediate action, work and the opportunity to put learning to use."
5. In this regard, international Education Commission put forth the view: "Non-formal education is a life-long process and it emphasises the informal and non-formal education for those, who left education at certain stage of life and now they have felt the necessity."
6. Harbulsm's view: "Non-formal education is the only means of filling the gap between the 'schooled' and "unschooled' population."

A few Characteristics of Non-Formal Education are as:

1. It is fully learner-centred approach because its convenience, needs and requirements of its surroundings are fully recognised here.
2. It is life-oriented and enviornment based. It enriches life with new experiences.
3. It catters to the needs and requirements of one and all. Learners in all walks of life and of every age group are able to receive eduation.
4. There is a good deal of flexibility to help the learners.
5. It develops positive attitude in the learners and thus helps them to become self-reliant.
6. In curriculum and methodology, there is too much of flexibility so as to encourage all types of learners.
7. It is an open system of education without any rigid rules and regulations.
8. There is a good deal of diversification of courses so as to benefit all types of learners.
9. It is a voluntary type of education provided through non-formal means.
10. It is continuing education and for this purpose appropriate facilities are created.

Advantages

1. One can earn while learning. One becomes self-dependent and self-confident.
2. Habit of hard work is developed.
3. There is proper use of leisure time. Usually the student of non-formal edcuatlon wants to use the free time in studies.
4. It helps the learners to achieve their goals of life. Even the fast changing goals are possible to be achieved.
5. Through non-formal education, one can cover up one's deficiency in any aspect and thus is able to improve one's standard of living.

Disadvantages

1. A student may receive the desired type of degree/ certificate diploma but many a time he does not enjoy full confidence as the regularly studied learner enjoys.
2. A student is not able to study regularly. He/she studies day and night near the examination and thus chance factor and luck play a good deal of role in his career.

Which Type of Education Do We Need More ?

Out of the formal, informal and non-formal types of education which is of greater significance for us or for the society? We can't say that we need more the formal type or our greater need is the informal type of education. Also we can't decidedly say that non-formal education is more significant. No individual can have all education in formal ways only or through informal ways only or through non-formal process of education. Whatever may both individual and whatever may be his/her environment, there is need of formal, informal and non-formal type of education. All these three types put together are able to bring about proper growth and development of the individual. So there is need of the three-one or two out of these can't be equivalent to the unfunctioning of the three put together.

Assignments

1. What do you mean by the term 'Education'?' How would you interpret education its narrower and loader sense?
2. Define Education and explain Indian and Western concepts of Education.
3. "Education is a natural, harmonious and progressive development of man's innate powers. Comment.
4. "By Education I mean an all round drawing out of the best in child and man-body, mind and spirit. Discuss.
5. Explain clearly the difference between formal, informal and non-format education by giving suitable examples.
6. How is non-formal education different from informal education? Write by giving suitable examples.

7. Write brief answer to the following:
   - (a) Give any definition of 'Education' and explain it.
   - (b) Differentiate between formal and non-formal education.
   - (c) Is there any difference between informal and non-formal education? Write briefly.

2

Objectives and Aims of Education

In every walk of life, aims are of unique importance. Without fixing up aims, the work that we take up remains dull and cheerless aims. In fact it makes the process lively, and they also provide satisfaction at the end. In the field of education aims are very essential. Undoubtedly, education is a purposeful and planned activity. It makes a man quite fit for the society. Therefore, we should try to fix up aims in advance and then make efforts to achieve them.

Education without an aim is quite meaningless. In the words of John Oewey, "An aim is a foreseen end that gives direction to an activity or motivates behaviour." An aim to predetermined goal which inspires the welfare activities of an individual, after careful thinking and proper planning it is achieved. In fact, an aim is that predetermined goal which stimulates human activities to achieve it.

The Criteria

1. They emerge out of the existing conditions.
2. They are tentative. They can be revised as per need and requirement.
3. They are well-defined.
4. They are flexible.
5. They are related to the life and aspirations of the people.

John Dewey suggested the following criteria for aims of education:

1. Good aims are related to real situations of life. They grow out of these situations and they can be achieved only under these situations.
2. Good aims are flexible. These should be flexible enough to meet the demands of changing circumstances of life.
3. A good aim represents a span of diverse activity. The real objective in pursuing an end is not the end itself but the course of the activity itself which constitutes the core of education.

Importance

There is a great importance of aimes of education. All scholars philosophers and educationists have laid great stress on the importance of aims in education. Being a systematic and planned activity, education loses much of its significance without clear-cut aims. According to Encyclopaedia of Modern Education, "Education is purposeful and ethical activity. Hence it is unthinkable without aims." in fact, without aims neither an individual nor an institution is capable of realising its potentialities."

Educational aims are important due to the following reasons:

1. Aims are necessary as they give direction to an act. Education is a planned activity. It has certain aims in view. The aim as a foreseen end as it gives direction to the education process. Without aims, the educator is like a sailor who does not know his destination and the pupil is like a rudderless vessel which may be drifted along somewhere ashore.
2. Aims allow us to act intelligently. John Dewey has aptly remarked, "Acting with an aim is all one with acting intelligently." Thus by keeping the aim in view, one knows what one is doing and why one is doing it. It saves wastage of time and energy.

3. Aims help in assessing the outcomes of the education process. They are necessary because they help in measuring the success and failure of work done in the school.
4. Aims are necessary for efficient school administration. They help the school authorities in organising, equipping and managing the school. This refers to the selection of teachers, curriculum, planning, proper library equipment, planning of various activities etc. Each activity is guided by educational aims.
5. Aims give direction to the work of the pupils. Once the pupils are clear about the aims, they are likely to co-operate and work with zeal for the achievement of these aims.
6. Aims are useful for parents and general public. Parents and general public can appreciate the work of the school in the light of aims. Aims put restraint on the undue criticism from the parents.
7. Aims give continuity and significance to education. Education is a continuous process. It has an intrinsic continuity. It is the aim that gives continuity and significance to the series of events and experiences that make up what we call education. So aims are potential seeds from which grows the plant of a well-defined educational policy. Aims help us in acting with meaning.

Nature of Aims

Aims are the core of a workable philosophy of education. Without philosophy, an educator could not have aims and without aims he could not have a practical philosophy.

Aims are an integral part of the fabric of the educative process. They enable an individual to continue his education. As such, an aim is not an end ; it is only a means to an end.

Aims are both within and without the educative process. Ward G. Reader rightly points out, "Education finds its aims both within and without the educative process. It must be kept in mind the interests and the abilities of the pupil and prepare him to share in democratic living both now and when he becomes an adult."

Determining Factors

Many factors contribute to the determining of educational aims. These factors touch every phase of human life and also reflect socio-cultural trends. The following factors usually determine aims of education :

1. **Philosophy of Life.** Aims of education have direct relationship with the prevailing philosophy of life. Different thankers and philosophical thoughts influence the course of education and its aims. Idealism emphasises self-realisation and divine perfection as the aims of education. According to the natural-view point, self-expression or self-gratification should be the aim of education. The pragmatic school of thought views life as the process of socialization of an individual. Similarly, existentialism, realism and other philosophical view points recommended their own aims of education.

2. **Human Nature.** Educational aims have often been decided keeping in view the human nature. Idealists regard 'unfolding the divine man' as the aim of education. To naturalists, the aim of education is "self-expression."

3. **Religious Factors.** Though there is no state religion in India, yet different religious view points influence the aims of education. The denominational institutions run by different religious organisations have to work to realise the goals accordingly.

4. **Political Ideology.** No system of education can rise above the political ideologies of the country. In other words, political ideologies influence aims of education in a significant way. According to Brown, "Education in any country and at points reflects value of the ruling class." Under a totalitarian system, the aims of education are different from those under a democratic political system.

Under a democratic set-up, the-aims of education are flexible. The goal of education is the good man who is to be educated for life of freedom. Education aims at developing the full personality of each individual, irrespective of caste, creed, class or religion.

Under a totalitarian system, the aim of education is to propagate the state ideology. It is, in fact, indoctrination. The good of the individual lies in his working for the good of the state. Thus he dies for the state.

5. Socio-Economic Problems. Socio-economic problems of a country determine the aims of education. In India, we have a number of socio-economic problems. One of the objectives of education may be to establish a socialistic pattern of society which is in tune with the democratic set-up of the country. Similarly, the educational system of the country is expected to produce socially and economically independent citizens who can contribute to the betterment of the country. In the words of Secondary Education Commission Report (1952-53) : "As political, social and economic conditions change and new problems arise, it becomes necessary to re-examine and re-state clearly the objectives which education at each definite stage, should keep in view."

6. Cultural Factors Socio-cultural heritage of a country largely determines the aims of education. Education has to preserve and develop the cultural heritage. The changing and developing pattern of culture directly influences the aims of education.

7. Exploration of Knowledge Present age is the age of science and technology. There is almost an explosion of knowldege. Education today, has become cience-oriented and technology-based. It is thus evident that exploration of knowledge is an important factor in determining the aims of education.

Education must represent these factors and be related to the realities and problems of life.

Different Aims at Different Times

Aims of Education as history reveals, differed from time to time. Here below are given the aims of education which were popularly advocated at different times:

Ancient India

1. To infuse in the learners piety and religiousness.

2. To form good character.
3. To develop the personality fully.
4. To inculcate civic and social duties.
5. To promote social efficiency and happiness.
6. To preserve and propagate culture.

In Medieval India

1. Propagation of islam.
2. Spread of education among Muslims.
3. Extension of islamic kingdom.
4. Development of morality.
5. Building of character.
6. Propagation of 'Shariyat'.
7. Achievement of material well being.

During the British Rule

1. Consolidation of British empire.
2. Recruitment of clerks.
3. Spreading English Literature.
4. Promoting craze for English articles and English textiles.
5. Preparing a class of interpreters of English laws.
6. Translating literary master pieces of Indian religious books into English.

Changing Aims

Aims of Education are related to time and space. They are also changeable. The history of educational development in India stands evidence to this fact. There have been different aims of education in different periods. A brief account of aims of education in chronological sequence is given below :

Aims of Education in the Brahmanic Period. The aim of education during Brahmanic period was an all-sided development of man. Education was regarded as a means of salvation or emancipation. The chief aim of education was to unfold the spiritual and normal power of the individual. Education was thus determined by religious values.

The Aims of Buddhist Education. The aim of education during Buddhist period was to create a sense of equality among all, 'Satya' and 'Ahimsa' were the directive principles of this system of education. The child was taught to control and suppress his worldly desires in accordance with the eightfold code of conduct enunciated by Lord Buddha.

Aims of Education during Muslim Rule. The aim of education during the Muslim period was to prepare an individual for the wordly life as well as for the spiritual life. It was education of islamic culture and scriptures which regulated human behaviour accordingly.

Aims of Education during British Rule. The aims of education during British rule were different. The system of British education was implanted in this country with purely political motives. It aimed at dividing Indians spiritually and intellectually into the English-knowing class of men and non-English-knowing masses of people. It was in accordance with Macaulay's "Downward Filtration Theory."

Aims in Emerging Society

Aims of Education need careful fixation. They have to be in accordance with the needs and requirements of the individuals, the society, the nation and the situations prevailing all around. Aims of education have been different at different times. After the independence of the country Pt. Jawahar Lal Nehru remarked, "Great changes have taken place in the country and the educational system must be keeping with them. The entire basis of education must be revolutionised." The society today is facing a number of problems. Social, political and economic conditions of the country are fast changing. It is, therefore, very important that we should assess everything carefully in the light of present situations and fix up aims of education which are suitable for the people of free India in every way. Suggested aims of education are :

1. Individual Aim of Education.
2. Social Aim of Education.
3. Vocational aim of Education.
4. Character Building Aim.
5. Spiritual Aim of Education.
6. Harmonious Development Aim.
7. Cultural Aim of Education.
8. Knowledge Aim of Education.

Individual Aims

Individual aim of education means that education should develop the individuals according to their interests and capabilities. It meas free growth of individuality, helping every boy and girl to achieve the highest degree of individual development. Individuality is the ideal of life. An individual is the central figure in the social setup of life. All social institutions exist for the betterment and improvement of the individual. The individual is the end and these social institutions are the means. It is the fullest development of the individual. Education aims at training and development of the individual. It is only this type of individual who comes out as a good citizen.

The individual aims of education have been emphasised by various thinkers. Their view points are as under:

The Naturalists like Rousseau believe that "The central aim of education is the autonomous development of the individual." According to him, "Everything is good as it comes from the hands of Author of Nature, but everything degenerates at the hands of man. God makes all things good. Man meddles with them and they become evil." This group of thinkers believe that man and citizen cannot be trained simultaneously. In short, education must secure those conditions where every individual is allowed to have a free play of his personality. He is free to develop his inherent, powers the highest potentialities of self.

The biologists believe that every individual *is* unique in his own way. G. Thompson believes that "Education is for the individual. Its function being to enable the individual to survive and live out its complete life. Education is imparted to preserve the individual life. Education is given for the sake of the individual to save him from destruction. Community exists for the individual, not the individual for the community. Community being the means and individual being the end, education should not set the means over the end." Therefore, individual and not society should be the centre of all educational efforts and activities.

According to the psychologists, education is an individual process. No two children are identical in intellectual capacity. Education must be individualised. Then only they can be benefitted fully.

The modern progressive thinkers also hold the view that the ultimate good of society lies in discovering the hidden value of the individual. In the words of Sir Percy Nunn, enters the human world except in end through the free activities of the individual men and women and that educational practice must be shaped to accord with the truth."

Each individual child should hold the key positions in the educative process. There is much force in the individual aim of education. However, individual aim, in its extreme form, is not desirable. The social aim has its own values and justification. This extreme and one-sided view of individual aims has teen criticised.

Criticism of Individual Aim of Education

The individual aim of education has been discussed on account of the following points:

Isolated Individual- a figment of imagination. "An isolated individual" as, T. Rayment says, "is only a figment of imagination. We cannot conceive of an individual living and developing in isolation from society."

An Individual is a Social Being. In the words of John Dewey, "As a social being he is a citizen growing and thinking in a vast complex of interactions and relations." So an educational activity that does not swear by the social end, consequently fails even to serve the individual.

Inherently Defective. The idea of autonomous development may be misinterpreted as giving absolute freedom to the individual. It may take the form of unchecked self-expression' or 'self-assertion.' If we ridlcute all social conventions or moral laws which form the basis of society. *Sir-fierey* Atowrngntly *sects.* Individuality develops only in a social atmosphere.

The critics of individual aims believe that the individual left to himself, is an animal, selfish and undisciplined. Thus it is against the spiritual nature of man.

Individual must be Made Fit for the Society. Rusk says that the aim of education is not development of individuality but the enrichment of personality. Education must transform him from individual being to social being. He must be fit to live in the society.

The Basis of Individual's greaters is Social. The contribution of great men (individual being?) wen not isolated from the society. Their greatness was due to their assi xlation of the rich Heritage of the society. They worked against some social background. Hence the very basis of their great contributions was social.

In all, individual aim of education in its extra form is one sided. It is not in tune with the socio-political set-up of the country. It may adversely affect the economy of the country as well. Those who believe in it are self-centred and perhaps selfish. It is all right to a limited extent. Society or state aim also very important.

Social Aims

A man in isolation is not considered good. He is known by the company he keeps or the society he belongs to. Surely the society or state is superior to the individual. That is my view-point of supporters of social aim of education.

In its extreme form, social aim regards individual only as a tool of society. He is subordinate to the society. Moreover, it cannot live without society.

Arguments in favour of Social Aim

Below are given the arguments of those who are in favour of social aim of education:

An Individual is an Integral Part of the Society. He is born in society and he grows and develops in society. Sodety should be given more importance as compared to the individual.

The Individual is Born with a Number of Raw Instincts. The society gives training to him. The good sodt environment makes him a man. Social environment need be cared for more as compared to the individual.

Education is Under the Control of the State. State or society is to determine 'what' and 'how' of education. What should be taught to the individual and how it should be taught are determined by the society. Therefore, social aim is more important.

Society Makes the Individual Civilized. It teaches him the lesson of citizenship. So the society or the social aims need be given more importance.

Security, Peace and Justice exist in Society. They are properly maintained in the society only. It is, therefore, urgently needed on the part of the individual that he should give importance to society.

Thus, we find that the social aim of education completely overpowers the individual.

Criticism of the Social Aim of Education

Social aim of education in its extreme form has been criticised in many ways. It is certainly one-sided view. The following are the points of criticism:

1. It is unpsychological bcecause it does not take into account the capacities and interests of the individual. Man becomes a means to an end. He has to sacrifice his own interests.

2. It suppresses individual freedom, develops narrow nationalism and ignores the individual completely, it leaves no scope for the individual personality to flourish.
3. It ignores the needs, desires and interests of the individual and also suppresses his creative power.
4. It tries to make the individual just a tool of the state. He forgets his own individuality and becomes a blind servant of the society.
5. The desires and aspirations of the individual are ended and he has to work for the good of the society. Thus education makes an individual a tool of the society. It may make the individual narrow-minded and in them there may develop all hatred for the society.

Synthesising Individual and Social Aims

Are individual aims of education sufficient in themselves? Can we go on fully with their support? No, it is not possible. An individual cannot be thought of in a vaccum. Support of the society is a must for him. He is an integral part of the society. We shall have to think of betterment of society through the increase of education. Education is a very good weapon to cut off the itching sharpness of individual and social aims of education. They have certain drawbacks and those must be ended. Then the two—individual and soda! aims of education be synthesised. Surety,they are contemporary nature. Each one wilt become a support for the other. That way then, they will serve the purpose in far better ways.

Synthesising the individual and social aims of education will create healthy and conducive environment which will ensure proper growth and development of the individual. There will be nothing bad for the individual no suppression of his creativeness. Better individual will give rise to a group of better individuals and that will naturally improve the society in every day.

Every individual has got the capacity to make the society grow and develop full. Everyone wants to see it prospering. For this achievement, the individual will have to be prepared for the self-sacrifice for the society. Education serves that purpose fruitfully. Education has two fold purpose : "The perfection of the individual and good of the community. Isolated individual is the figment of imagination.

An individual is like a plant and society is the soil or earth. No plant can grow in the absence of soil or earth. Social medium is needed for the proper growth of the individual. In the words of John Adam "individuality requires a social medium to grow, without social contacts we are not human." According to Ross, "individuality is of no value and personality is a meaningless term, apart from the social-environment in which they are developed and made manifest. Self-reallsation can be achieved onty through social services and the social-ideas of real value can come into being only through free individuals who have developed valuable individuality. The circle cannot be broken."

There is no conflict between self-realisation and social service as aim of life. It is, undoubtedly, right to say that the true aim of education is the highest development of the individual as a member of the society.

A few experts gave their views to favour it :

(i) Adams, "Self is realised in society through social interaction."

(ii) Maclver, "Socialization and individualisation are two sides of a single process."

(iii) Nunn says, "individuality develops only in a social atmosphere where it can feed on common interests and common activities."

(iv) in the words of Mahatma Gandhi, Gandhi sees no conflict between individual and society. He says, "I believe that if one man gains spiritually, the whole world gains with him."

(v) According to Humayun Kabir: "If one is to be creative member of society, one must not sustain one's own growth, but contributes something to the growth of society."

Thus we find that both the individual and the society are needed for making life full of fragrance and worthy of living. Initiative of the individual is important at its own place and social contact is needed to give the individual proper recognition and right-direction. Both supplement each other. So by synthesizing the two we shall be able to make the individual and the society grow and develop fully.

Vocational Aims

Livelihood is important because without bread and butter, living is not possible. Education, therefore, must enable an individual to stand on his own feet and he should be able to earn for his living. Only a living person has certain needs and requirements. A dead person has no desire, no aspiration and no requirements. When we talk of a living person, we surely see to it from his all around point of view. An individual needs education in order to live. He needs education in order to live well. He needs education to do various things of life in a better way. They are possible with the help of money only. According to Secondary Education Commission, knowledge gained is useless if an individual cannot make both ends meet. Without a vocation, the individual is a drag and parasite on others. A social parasite cannot be called a free man. He begins to feel free only when he is economically independent. Vocational education, thus, exercises a liberalising effect on man. There is no vocation without education. Every vocation has an educational value. Education with the vocational aim in the background will prepare each individual for an occupation. Vocational aim of education is also known as 'Bread and Butter aim', 'Blue Jacket Aim' and 'White Collar Aim.'

It has been rightly said that "Vocational Education is an education of most effective kind, for lack of which those who merely go to school, suffer all their lives." in the words of Gandhiji, "True education ought to be a kind of insurance against unemployment."

Merits of Vocational Aims

Solves Economic Problems. Vocational aims make a person fit for some vocation. He becomes sound economically. In this age of material crisis, the problem of unemployment and underemployment are causing many economic problems. When education is vocation centred, it will help a lot.

Gives Social Status. Vocational aims bring vocational efficiency. With more money, a person feels satisfied in the society. It gives him good social status.

Suits the Average Learners. In every classroom, there are different types of learners. The good and brilliant are able to do well in studies. But the average types of learners find studies a big problem. Vocational education helps them, because it is suitable for them.

Helps in Moral Development. In the absence of vocation centred education, many students would become misfit for society. They will do every type of bad deeds to earn money for their living. Vocational education thus makes them morally good.

Makes a Person Active. In vocational education, the learners are able to develop their interests in the vocation. Quite a number of them are able to excel.

Makes Learning Useful. Vocational education makes learning useful. Here some vocation is of primary importance. The study of so-called traditional subjects is secondary.

A few experts pirt-forth their views as under:

Spens Report, "Preparation for vocation is an important part of our education."

Hartshome's view, "Vocational education is an education of most effective kind, for lack of which those who merely go to school, suffer all their lives."

Demerits

1. Only vocational aim is not sufficient for an individual. Some studies are also needed. Social and cultural aims are in no way of lesser importance.
2. It is a narrow aim of education.
3. It is too much materialistic.

It we have a professionally good doctor or a professionally good engineer, it is not sufficient. There is need of a good man in each one of them. So just vocational aim is not sufficient. All other aims which make an individual a good person, are also fleeced.

Character Building Aims

Character is very important in the case of every learner, every teacher, every professional and above all, every person. In the absence of a good character, the whole personality stands zeroed. It is the soul of human body. Education for character is of top-most importance. It gives the man confidence and courage. A man of character is a man of word, is a true national, is a true citizen, and above all, a true human-being. India needs today men of character. In them lie the hope and future prosperity of the nation. Only persons of character make the nation great and strong.

In the present day life, when there are erosion of higher values, education for character is the only way to solve the problems. Definitely the society of today is badly in need of higher values of life—Truth, Beauty and Goodness.

The chief aim of education should be 'character building.' Herbart summed up the concept of education as 'Morality.'

Swami *Vivekanand* says, "We want that education by which character is formed, strength of mind, is increased, the intellect is expanded and by which one can stand on one's own feet."

John Dewey says, "The establishing of character is a comprehensive aim of school instruction and discipline."

Raymont says, "The teacher's ultimate concern is to cultivate, not wealth or muscle, nor fulness of knowledge, nor refinement of feeling, but strength and purity of character."

'Gandhiji very dearly said, "Character building is the aim of education. I would try to develop courage, strength, virtue the ability to forget onself in working towards great aims. I should feel that if we succeed in building the character of individual, society will take care of itself."

in the words Radhakrishannan, "The troubles of the whole world including India and the fact that education has become a mere intellectual exercise and not the acquisition of moral and spiritual values."

How can Education help in Character Building?

Personal Examples of Teachers and Administrators. The teachers and the Administrators working in the schools should be living good examples of character. The learners come in contact with them every now and then and they observe them and watch them carefully at every moment. Only good teaching personnels will be able to imbibe the qualities of good character in the learners.

Encourage the Students to Read' Good Books. The teachers should recommend the study of good books to the students. Biographies of great men were really great in the true sense of the word should be purchased for the library. Such books should be within easy access of the students. Then naturally the students will read those books and learn lesson for all times to comes.

Moral Education as a Subject. Moral education as a subject should be introduced in the school curriculum. The different textbooks of all subjects of among or more education as a subject among me youths will naturally improve upon their moral behaviour. The earlier we start with this, the better it would be for the future of society and the nation.

Celebration of Birth Days. The school should actually celebrate the birthdays of great religious leaders and saints. Instead of declaring a holiday on such days, celebration of the day highlighting the achievements and contributions of those great men will help the learners to learn many good things. Naturally it will improve upon their moral behaviour.

Projects for Honesty. A few projects for honesty may be started in the school. Students' Post Office, Students' Co-operative Store, Students' Canteen etc. may be started. The students should be given the charge of these activities under the guidance of some teacher and they should run it on 'No Profit, No Loss' basis. This will imbibe in the students qualities like sincerity, honesty and hardwork which will make them an asset for the society.

Lectures by Persons of High Moral Values. Some religious persons who are really saints of the society should be invited to the school for a lecture on moral education. Speech by them based on their studies and experiences of life will create interest in the students and also help them in becoming morally better students.

Merits

1. A person without character is like a man with body and without soul. So character building aim of education is really of primary importance.
2. Everybody needs be good human being. That is not possible without character. Therefore, character building as aim of education should be given top-most importance.

Demerits

1. Let there are not too much moral values. If we do so, other aspects of life stand neglected.
2. What is good and what is bad need to be known to everyone. Character aim is moral and that is for all. In its absence, it will be difficult to live well in a social group.

Cultural Aims

Education for culture is education to improve upon cultural aspect of the society. That improvement can be there only it we have the past and the present cultures available with us many good things we want to preserve, we want to refine and transmit in order to enrich our culture all the more. Cultural aspect of life is significant in its own way.

Cultural aim in narrow sense means dress, manners, way of life etc. In broader sense, it means good habits; good thoughts, etc. Surely cultural aim of education is grace to human life. Humanyun Kabir has rightly emphasised the importance of culture in the words : The continuity of culture and traditions is an essential condition for the survival of a nation" Culture is the foundation, the pifthary thing—it should snow itself in the smallest detail of your conduct and personal behaviour, how you sit, how you talk, how you dress, etc, inner culture must be reflected in your speech, the way in which you treat visitors and guests and behave towards one another and your teachers and elders.'

A few definitions of Cultures

1. Ottaway, The culture of society means the total way of life of a society.
2. Mettfww Arnold said, The best that has been thought and know is culture."
3. Ellwood, "Culture includes on the one hand the whole of man's material civilisation, tools, weapons, systems of industry, and on the other, all the non-material or spiritual civilisation such as language literature, art, morality, law and Government."
4. In the words of E.B Taytor, "Culture is that complex whole which includes knowledge, belief art, moral law, custom and any other capabilities and habits acquired by man as a member of society."

Merits

1. One comes to know about all the things then one can transmit or preserve them better.
2 One can improve one's culture update it in the light of other cultures.
3. A person culturally more sound is one who excels in one aspect, gains confidence and that helps to becoming better or other aspects of personality.
4. It adds grace to human. We, make it worth living as there is a keen desire to prosper, to flourish and to live-better and better.
5. It glorifies the nation, enriches its already rich cultural heritage.
6. One is able to understand society properly and can add to enrich it and can also root out ills from it. One can also eliminate the bad elements from the culture.
7. It trains and cultivates human powers. John Dewey said

that an individual is enabled to join freely and fully in shared or common activities.

Demerits

1. Too much emphasis on cultural aim will lead to neglect or other aspects of personality.
2. It will be in line with the surrounding and the prevailing social climate.
3. It hinders the natural development of the child. In the words of T.P. Nunn, "the aim of cultural-development-hinders a child from developing according to his own interests and potentialities." He further says, "National institutions and traditions have a performance which made individual life a trivial thing."
4. A few bad things cannot be allowed to continue but in cultural aim that has to be continued. Long and fellow gap stated "Let the past bury its dead"
5. It leads to neglect of professional aspect of education which is very important to earn one's livelihood.
6. There are many cultures in the world which one is ideal and the best—it is difficult to decide, if we go on within our own culture, our vision may be narrow and may be too low.

Cultural aim of education is important but it cannot be given priority in the aims of education. It can surely assist the other aims with some broader thinking on it. In the words of Rafifidm Pwad, "India has to choose for herself a culture that derives inspiration from what is noble in our ancient culture and at the same time does not ignore demands of the present age."

Spiritual Aims

Education makes a person spiritually sound. A person who is spiritually sound behaves better. He/she is able to do well while being trained for social efficiency, sound moraly and physical betterment. In the absence of spiritual aha of eduction, one's life is incomplete. Spiritual aim is the pillar on which rests the edifice of total personality. Surely it is deeply linked wtth the character building aim. Spiritual aim gives strength to human soul and mind. The great spiritualists like Guru Nanak, Buddha, Mahavir, Swami Dayanand, Vivekanand, Shankaracharya, Aurobindo, Gandhi, Tagore accepted the spiritual aim of education. Views of some of them on this aspect of life are given below and they are worth mentioning down:

Aurobindo said, "Every man has in himself something divine, something his own, a chance of perfection and strength. In however small a sphere which God offers him to take or refuse. The task is to find it, develop it and use it. The chief aim of education should be to help the growing soul to draw out that in self which is best and make it perfect for a noble cause.

Finfey said, "Material progress is good thing; social and political reforms are mere valuable both to the race and the individual; their final worth lies in the aid they afford to spiritual life."

Radhakrishnan said, "The aim of education is neither national efficiency, nor world solidarity, but making the individual feel that he has within himself something deeper than intellect, call it spirit. If you like."

Merits

1. Spiritual aim of education makes a person gentle and pious.
2. It makes the students religious minded. They are able to have some values of life—and all this has its good effect on their behaviours.
3. It makes the personality of the individual strong. He/she becomes a man of character, honesty and integrity.
4. It reduces the problems of indiscipline, conflicts, quarrels to some extent corruption, greed, aggression etc., destruction, hatred are on the increase. All these also stand checked to a considerable extent.

Demerits

1. One may think of leaving the worldly life. That is not so good for every one.
2. Spiritual aim may be achieved but one may not be so practical.

Spiritual aim of education, no doubt, is important but it cannot be given top-most priority in the aim of education. Other aims of education the vocational aim, knowledge aim, etc will to be cared for fully. Then and then and then only it will remain practical and useful to lead a good life in the society.

Harmonious Development Aim

Harmonious development of personality is considered to be the main aim of education. In harmonious development, various facets of personality i.e. academic, social, cultural, economic, spiritual, aesthetic etc. are fully cared for and they are given equal importance. Emphasis on all aspect of personality helps to have a balanced type of personality. In the process of education, different types of education are important in their own ways. Each one has great significance. None of them should be ignored considering it insignificant. One of them or two out of them should not be considered more important than others. Due recognition to each aim and that also on proportionate basis must be given. Then only there will be harmony in the various aspects of an individual's personality. A harmoniously developed individual is an asset not only to the social group or community but also to the society or the nation he belongs to. He is good, incarnate and he is bound to emit fragrance and imbibe in others goodness wherever he is and wherever he goes. Therefore, harmonious development aim of education is important and it must be properly attended to by one and all.

The great men say so about harmonious development aims

Rousseau regards education as, "The process of development into an enjoyable, rational, harmoniously-balanced, useful and hence natural life."

In the words of Ross, "Harmonious development needs the intellectual, religious, moral and aesthetic development of the child."

Pestalozzi says, "Education is natural, harmonious and progressive development of man's innate powers." By harmonious development, he means the education of head, heart and hand.

In this context Gandhiji said, "By education I mean an all round drawing out of the best in child and man—body, mind and spirit," He further says, "Man is neither mere intellect, nor the gross animal, nor the heart and soul alone. A proper and harmonious combination of all the three is required for the making of the whole man and constitutes the true economics of education."

Merits

1. An individual comes out all round good. He is successful in whatever type of situation he is placed.
2. He is academically good, physically and mentally sound, normally and culturally all right, has social efficiency and is economically a fit person for some vocation.
3. It is complete living. It makes an individual useful and self-reliant person.

Demertis

1. Development of all aspects is not possible fully in one way or the other, one may lag behind.
2. It is not possible to measure accurately whether the desired ends are reached or not.
3. Individual differences are always there.
4. Harmonius development aim is goodwithin this age of competitions where only academic aspect is the main criteria, the person may not get a chance of selection.
5. In some institutions, all facilities for harmonious development of personality are not available. Moreover, it is very difficult to decide a suitable curriculum for it.

6 The problems of population explosion, unemployment hinder the harmonious development of the individual.

Knowledge Aim

Knowledge is very important these days. A person with good and uptodate knowledge is able to impress others. Such a person gets applaud wharever he is and wherever he goes. Education equips a person with adequate knowledge. It updates his knowldge aim of education. Is it the most important aim of education? The answer to this has to be thought of carefully. Knowledge is not the only thing important in life. An individual stands adorned with knowledge. Apart from academic aspect, other aspects of personality i.e. physical aspect, social, cultural, moral, educational are in no way of lesser importance. One thing is definite that knowledge about social, cultural, moral aspects is possible only if one has acquired the knowledge. That way knowledge aim may be called a foundational one. Socrates said, "One who had tre knowledge should not be other than virtuous."

Merits

The following are the merits of knowledge aim of education:

1. It is a very good instrument of education.
2. It helps the individual in making adjustment in life.
3. It helps the individual as well as the society in the proper growth and development.
4. It strengthens morality.
5. It makes an individual thoughtful.
6. It serves as a means to achieve some end.

Demerits

1. Knowledge for the sake of knowledge is not good.
2. More knowledge is good but it is add out the cost of starving the soul.

Aims of education must be related to the needs and requirements of the people. In this fast changing age when values of life are changing, life is becoming complex and to live well is a challenge for everyone. Education should equip a person to face life boldly and courageously, eradicate its shortcomings and make it worthy of living. Education must enable an individual to come out all successful in every walk of life whatever may be the situation— political, social, cultural and whatever may be the circumstances of the individual. Then and then only education will be called education worth the name—an instrument of utility and usefulness for humanity.

Aims of Education as Recommended by the Secondary Education Commission (1953)

The Commission made a bold statement in respect of aims of education for democratic India. It stated that education must develop in its citizens habits, attitudes, and qualities of character and equip them to bear the burden of life in the changing economic structure. The Commission suggested the following aims of education :

Development of Democratic Citizenship. It is the major responsibility of education to carefully train every citizen for democratic citizenship. Such a training comprises of:

Clear Thinking. Education should equip the individual with the capacity of clear thinking. The individual should be a good democratic citizen who is clear of head and clear at heart. This makes him have clear thinking about everything.

Receptive to New Ideas. The individual becomes open minded. He welcomes new ideas at every stage. He is not a narrow thinking individual tied to the old customs and traditions. He is always willing to accept the change.

Clearness in Speech and Writing. The individual has clarity in speech and in writing. While exchanging ideas with others orally, he remains peaceful. While writing maintains clarity and is able to present ideas with full clarity.

Trúe Patriotism. The individual is a true patriot through and through. He leaves narrow ideology of selfishness in the interest of broaded national feelings. He is well-wisher of a nation and whatever he does or says, he remains in tune with the nation.

Art of Living with the Community. The individual learns to live with others. He believes in co-operation and co-existence. He is a social being ever-ready to learn the art of living with community.

Development of Internationalism. Education imbibes the qualities of world citizenship. He believes in universal brotherhood. Today just patriotism is not sufficient. There is need of true and pure nationalism which believes in internationalism.

Improvement of Vocational Efficiency. Education must aimed at increasing the productive or vocational efficiency of young students. It includes :

(a) Realisation of the national prosperity is possible only through work.

(b) A new attitude toward work and dignity of labour.

The emphasis should be on crafts and productive work and diversification of courses. The ideas is that a large number of students may take up vocational courses.

Development of Personality. Education should develop Htence, artistic and cultural interests of the students. These are necessary for self-expression and for the full development of human personality. For this purpose subjects like art, craft, music, dancing etc should be included in the scheme of studies.

Education for Leadership. In order o make democracy function successfuHy, it is essential' To' incutctr - the qualities of leadership in youth. Education should train the youth to provide leadership in the social, poflfical, industrial and Itural fields.

Recommendations of Indian Education Commission regarding Aims Education (1964-66)

Indian Education Commission (1964-66) has made very valuable recommendational regarding the aims of education. It has, in fact, turned to refer to the whote system of education through its recommendations, the Commission has stated, "No reform is more urgent than to transform education, endeavour tb relate it to the life, neiptfs and-aspirations of the people' and thereby make it a powerful instalment of social, economic and cultural transformation, necessary for the realization of our-national goals."

The Commission is suggested the following aims of education for the purpose of reforming it :

1. Increasing Productivity
2. Promoting Social and National integration.
3. Accelerating the process of Modernisation.
4. Cultivating social, moral and spiritual values.

The details of these aims are given below :

Increasing Productivity

It is very essential to increase the productivity of a country in order to ensure its progress. This objective can be achieved by education. The commission has suggested to act upon the following programmes in order to achieve this goal:

Imparting Science Education. Imparting Science Education is very essential in modern age in oroer to increase productivity. Hence science should be made a compulsory subject from the school Stage upto the University stage. Science Education must "become an integral part of school education and uttimatety some study of science should become a part of all courses in the humanities and social sciences at the university stage."

Work Experience. It is very essential to include work experience in school curriculum in order to produce interest in work. Every student should have experience of doing some work from the early school stage. Hence practical experience should be given to the students at school, home, workshop, factory etc. so that skilled workers are available in the field of work and there is a definite increase in productivity of the country. The Commission also suggested that a student should be given a certificate only when he fulfils the condition of work experience.

Application of Science to Production Process. There is a great need of connecting the knowledge of science with the activities of productivity. Modern age is the age of machines. Productivity can be increased to a great extent by the use of machines and machines can be used efficiently only with the application of technical knowledge and the knowledge of science. Hence it is essential to include these elements of science in curriculum which can accelerate the action of productivity.

Vocationalization of Education. It is very essential to impart vocational education in order to fulfil the aim of increasing productivity. Hence there should be arrangement of vocationalization of education from the secondary school stage. The students should be given the required information and guidance for the proper selection of vocation so that they are able to choose the right vocation which is according to their interests and aptitudes and which can fulfil the needs of the country.

Promoting Social and National integration.

Indian Education Commission described the promotion of social and national integration as the main objective of education because the unity of the nation is the only solid basis of the strength of a country. The Commission recommended the following steps to be taken for this purpose :

Common Schools. There should be common schools for all students, belonging to any category or community.

Accelerating the Process of Modernization

There is a great need of continuous progress in the country so that we should be able to walk side by side with other countries of the world. Hence there is an urgent need of accelerating the process of modernization in our country so that we may be able to stand in line with the developed countries of the world. For this purpose, there is a great need for the use of science based on technical education. There is also a need for preserving and re-evaluating the cultural heritage of our country so that we may be able to move forward in every field of life.

The commission has given the following suggestions for this purpose :

(i) Education should create the feeling of curiosity and investigation through the development of proper interests, sentiments and attitudes. There is also a need for developing the power of dear thinking and decision-making in the students.

(ii) Education should create perfect intelligentsia which should be associated with the different categories of people and which should have deep roots in the soil of the country.

Cultivation of Social, Moral and Spiritual Values

Indian Education Commission had laid great emphasis on cultivating social, moral and spiritual values In order to associate education with Indian Culture Religious or moral education has always enjoyed a great importance in India. Everyone in this country wants that education should cultivate good qualities, moral values and spiritual understanding among the students so that they may cultivate these good qualities in other persons. The Commission has given the following suggestions in this connection.

(i) There should be an arrangement in the school time table for teaching fundamental principles of all religions.

(ii) The knowledge of becoming a good citizen should be made a part of education.

(iii) Social, moral, religious and spiritual qualities should be developed in students through practical working in the school.

Critical Evaluation of the Present System of Education

We should try to make a critical evaluation of the present system of education in the light of the aims of education suggested by the Indian Education Commission. The critical evaluation reveals to us the following things :

1. The present system of education has proved itself to be quite unsuccessful in creating good citizens. The standard of citizenship is falling day by day in our country because of the spread of corruption and indiscipline. And in general, there is fall in moral values.

2. Vocational education is not being given in the planned way in our country. No doubt, vocational education has been started in some schools, but the students are not given proper guidance in the selection of suitable vocations. They are not given any information of the opportunities of employment in various vocations.

3. Unsuccessful in Creating all Round Development. The present system of education in our country is quite unsuccessful in creating all round development in students. Our education lays great stress on intellectual development only. It ignores physical, economic, social and cultural development of the students.

4. Our education has also been unsuccessful in cultivating moral values in the students. As a result of it, moral standard of people is falling day by day Many persons in the country have become selfish and greedy.

5. No religious education is given to the students in our schools. As a result of it love for all religions has disappeared in our country and fanaticism has become the order of the day.

6. Our education has proved itself to be unsuccessful in developing national unity. Our teachers and education have not been able to convey the concept of national unity to the students. Nothing has been done to establish common schools in India as suggested by Indian Education Commission. The students belonging to various religions are not given opportunities to work together freely. Hence our students have not understood and developed the concept of national unity.

Ideal Aims of the Present Time

Following are the ideal aims of education at the present time :

1. All round or perfect development of the personality of all the students.
2. Creating good citizens out of all the students.
3. Imbibing the spirit of patriotism in the students.
4. Preparing students for the service of humanity.
5. Enabling the students to preserve their cultural heritage.
6. Cultivating the spirit of social and national unity in the minds of students.
7. Imparting vocational education for enabling the students to earn their livelihood.
8. Making proper use of Human Resources.
9. Giving moral, religious and spiritual education to students in order to raise their moral, and ethical standards.
10. Creating awareness in the minds of the students for modernization.

National Policy of Education (1986) on Aims of Education

National Policy of Education aims at National System of Education which implies that upto a given level, all students, irrespective of caste, creed, location or sex, have access to education of a comparable quality. (1) Common Educational Structure i.e. 10+2+3 (ii) National Computer frame work with a common core and other flexible components. All educational program are to be carried on in strict conformity with secular values.

Life Long Education. Education is a like long process. Naturally it is to continue once it has been started. Education will be provided to one and all. Universal literacy will be spread. Every person, whatever may be his profession and whatever occupation he may be engaged in, will be provided with the type of education he/she is interested in. Open school, open university, distance education centre, pace learning etc. will be provided.

Development of Manpower. The country needs manpower at different levels and in different areas of working. Education will develop suitable type of manpower of all type. Thus, it will help the country to grow and develop fully. Efforts will be to have national self-reliance.

Peaceful Co-existence. Education should help everyone believe in peaceful ways of life. It will, therefore, propagate national unity and international brothehood. All types of emotional integration will be aimed at. Mutual give and take policy, respect and regards for each other etc. will be inculcated in the people. India has always worked for peace and understanding between nations, treating the whole world as one family. True to this tradition, education has to strengthen this world view and motivate the younger generations for international cooperation and peaceful co-existence

Development of Socialism, Secularism and Democracy. Goals of socialism, secularism and democracy enshrined in our Constitution will be developed. Education will make everybody have scientific temperament, free and independent mind and.thinking Education has the accelerating role. This aim of development includes materialistic'as well as spiritualdevelopment. Education while helping in social development of all persons, leads them to, socialism, broadmindedness and democracy. It also includes economic development and political development. It aims at raising the standard of living of all persons.

Moral and ethical Values. Then being erosion of values in the social set-up of life, everything has to be geared up through the process of education. Value crisis has to be thwarted with the help of a suitable type of education. There is need of inculcating in the youth moral and ethical values from the beginning. 3asic values of life have to be incorporated in the school curriculum.

All Round Development. Education should help in bringing about all round development in the personality of the child. There should be physical, moral, social, cultural, academic development and thus an individual should be made a fit person for the Indian society who is not liable to go astray in anyway. All round development will include material and spiritual development.

Removal of Disparities. National Policy on Education lays special emphasis on the removal of disparities and equalising educational opportunities by attending to the specific needs of those who have been denied equality so far. It removes the following disparities in the field of education:

Education for Women's Equality. Eduction will be used as an agent of basic change in the status of women. In order to neutralise the accumulated inequalities, there will be well-conceived edge in favour of women. The National Education System will play a positive rote in the education of women. It would foster the development of new values through redesigned curricula, text-books, the training and orientation of women teachers and the active-involvement of education, institutions. Woman's education will be promoted as a part of various course and education stituations encouraged to take up active programme to further the cause of women's development through education.

Education of Scheduled Castes. The central focus in educational development of Scheduled Castes is their equalisation with the non-scheduled caste population at all stages of education. Following measures are contemplated for this purpose :

(a) Scholarship Schemes for Children of Scheduled Caste. Scholarship schemes will be adopted for children of Scheduled Castes from Class-1 upto Metric in order to improve their prospects of receiving essential education.

(b) Provision of facilities for Scheduled Caste students in students' hostels at district headquarters.

(c) Recruitment of teachers from Scheduled Castes.

(d) Location of school building, Balwadis and Adult Education Centres in such a way so as to facilitate full participation of the children of scheduled castes.

Other Educationally Backward Sections and Areas

Minorities. Some minority groups are educationally deprived or backward. Greater attention will be paid to the education of these groups in the interest of equality and social justice. This will naturally include the constitutional guarantees given to them to establish and administer their own educational institutions and protection to their language and culture.

Education for Handicapped. The objectives is to integrate physically and mentally handicapped with the general community as equal partners in order to prepare them for normal growth and to enable them to face life with courage and confidence. The following measures will be taken in this regard:

(a) Whenever it is feasible, the education of children with minor handicaps will be common with that of others.

(b) Special schools with hostets will be provided at district headquarters for the severely handicapped children.

(c) Adequate arrangements will be made to give vocational training to the disabled.

(d) Teacher's training programmes will be renovated to deal with the special difficulties of the handicapped children.

(e) Voluntary efforts for the education of the disabled will be encouraged in every possible way.

Adult Education. The whole nation must pledge itself to the eradication of illiteracy, particularly in the 15-35 age group. The Central and State Governments, political parties and their organisations, the mass media and educational institutions must commit themselves to mass literacy programmes of diverse nature. It will also have to involve, on a large scale, teachers, students, youths, voluntary agencies, employees etc. The mass literacy programme will also include functional knowledge and skill and also awareness among learners to improve their socio-economic condition.

Conclusion

Different commissions and committees have put forth suggestions regarding the aims of education suitable for contemporary Indian society. The different aims must be assessed in the light of needs and requirements of the individuals as well as that of the society. Fast changing trends of life should also be viewed and reviewed so as to reach the right type of conclusions. The emerging era being an age of science and technology and the futurity of the emerging society should not be overlooked. In their true perspectives, suitable and very apt aims of education only should be well tested and that way research based conclusions be arrived at and put to use for maximum benefit to the whole humanity.

Assignments

1. "Aim is foreseen end which gives direction to an activity." How far is this statement of John Dewey applicable to the field of education ?
2. Discuss the importance of 'aims of education". What are the factors which affect aims of education ?
3. "Individual and Social aims of education are the two aspects of the same process." Discuss.
4. What are the specific aims of education in India of to-day ? Which of these do you think is the most important and why?
5. What in your opinion should be the ideal aims of education at the present time ? How far do these ideal aims tally with the aims of education as recommended by Indian Education Commission ?
6. Name a few important aims of education and discuss any one aim in details.
7. Discuss individual or social aims of education fully.
8. (a) What is an aim of education ?

   (b) What is the criteria of good aims ?

   (c) Discuss any two factors which help in determining educational aims?

3

Definition, Nature and Scope of Philosophy

The word, Educational Philosophy comprises of two words i.e. education and philosophy. In fact, the two words are interlinked, inter-related and inter independent. The hard fact is that we cannot have education without philosophy. To think of philosophy without education is also not possible. The two seem to be very much close and in many ways associated with each other. Let us see to it.

Usually we find that almost every person is thinking about something at every moment. This is now very common in the present day set up of life which is becoming complex and it has more and more problems. The human beings remain in thoughtful moods. Are they philosophers? They are surely to some extent. That way every contemplating type of person may be called a philosopher. Who is then the real philosopher? The person who goes on thinking more and more, is curious to think further and further, goes on adding up to his knowledge may be called a philosopher.

Meaning of Philosophy

Philosophy ordinarily means a set of beliefs, religious or secular, in accordance with which one tries to live. Sometimes we hear students saying that such and such person is a philosopher. The teacher gives the example of a philosopher type boy. The philosopher is a self-centred man, being so much with this ownself that at times he is considered to be lost in his own thoughts. Undoubtedly, philosophy is a view and a way of life.

What is Philosophy ?

Philosophy is the oldest and original discipline. We may call it as the mother of all the firts and the science of all sciences. In Sanskrit, philosophy is known as "barshan' which means knowledge of reality. The word Ida'rshah' comes from the word 'Drish' which means to see. Thus true knowledge can be received by 'seeing'. Philosophy is the never ending thirst for knowledge. It is a method of thinking. It answers the ultimate questions of life.

The term 'philosophy' has been derived from the Greek words 'Philos and 'Sophia which respectively mean 'love' and of wisdom'. Thus philosophy means love of wisdom. That way any lover of wisdom could be called a philosopher. The simple reason being that philosophy is a search for knowledge and wisdom. In this regard, Plato stated. He who has a taste for every sort of knowledge and who is anxious to learn and is never satisfied may be just termed a philosopher. The philosopher is thoughtful remains in a thoughtful mood, being in search of new ideas, new knowledge with the help of his growing wisdom. The philosopher looks at different things in his own peculiar ways. With him and through him, ordinary and routine type of things may not remain so, they may rather be philosophised. The subject matter of phllosphical inquiry is the reality itself. Here the search of the philospher is for understanding Man, Nature and the Universe. The different fields of philosophy are educational philosophy. Social philosophy, Moral philosophy, Economic Philosphy, Political Philosophy etc. And the different philosophical approaches are Idealism, Naturalism, Pragmatism, Marxism, Existentialism, Materialism and so on.

Philosophy varies from individual to individual from place to place and from time to time. Thus different persons having their different ideologies, ways of life, tend to have different type of philosophies. Aldous Huxley rightly says in his work 'Ends and Means', "Every human being has a philosophy of his own, good or bad, high or low, purely individual or common with others." The world famous religious teachers like Lord Buddha, personal salvation. Jesus Christ advocated the philosophy of love and charity. Mohammed upheld the doctrine of brotherhood. Philosophy varies from rurals and tribals to those living in cities. The Americans being practical type and Britishers being more or less theoretical type have different philosophies of life. And then philosophy varies from time to time. Once authoritarian philosophy was very much in vogue but now with the lapse of time, democracy is the way of life and democratic philosophy is becoming popular philosophy of the people.

1. According to Henderson, It is "a search for a comprehensive view of nature, an attempt at a universal explanation of nature of things."
2. According to Curtis, "During the course of centuries, the meaning attached to philosophy has undergone many changes, and even at present day, thinkers are not in complete agreement about the aims and subject matter of this branch of knowledge."
3. Fichte's view, "Philosophy is the science of knowledge."
4. Coleridge defined philosophy as the "science of sciences."
5. Cisero said, "Philosophy is the matter of all arts and the true medicine of mind."
6. R.W. Seller says, "Philosophy is a persistent attempt to gain insight into the nature of the world and of ourselves by means of systematic reflection."
7. According to Bertrand Russell, the great British philosopher, "Philosophy like all other studies, aims primarily at knowledge."
8. In the words of Bramold : "Philosophy is a persistent effort of both ordinary and persistent people to make life as intelligible and meaningful as possible."
9. Kant says, "Philosophy is the science and criticism of cognition."
10. Adious Huxley remarked, "Men live in accordance with their philosophy of life, their conception of the world."
11. According to Aristippus, "Philosophy is the ability to feel at ease in any society."
12. Harold Titus said, "A person's philosophy is the sum of his fundamentals beliefs and convictions."

13. According to Prof. V.R. Taneja, "Philosophy being a mother discipline, all arts and sciences look to it for the solution of their problems."
14. Dr. Prem Nath says, "Philosophy is open-mindedness cultivated through the rigorous discipline of the mind."

In India, philosophy or Darshan is considered to be of great importance because it helps in guiding the destiny of human life. According to Dr. Radhakrishnan, "It is a logical inquiry into the nature of reality." Every human being on this earth has certain faiths, beliefs, values, way of life and in the course of his living on this earth, he goes on adding, subtracting, modifying some of them and in some cases, many of them adjusting themselves accordingly. Thus philosophy paves a way of life for an individual and his life in turn thereto helps in carving his philosophy best suited to him.

Characteristics

A few characteristics of philosophy are:

1. Philosophy is a living force.
2. It is a way of life.
3. It is the oldest and original discipline of thought.
4. It is a search for truth and reality.
5. It is based on inquiry about life and existence.
6. It is logical in its approach.
7. It is ever growing and developing.

Different Branches

Nature of Reality. What is this Universe. What is real on this earth? Such problems are dealt with by Metaphysics which is a branch of philosophy

Nature of Knowledge. Problems about real and unreal, truth and falsehood crop up Philosophy helps in giving this knowledge. This branch of philosophy is known as 'opis-temotogy'.

Nature of Values. Problems of different values in life exist. One branch of philosophy deals wtih it that philosophy is known as Axiology

Philosophy of Education has certain ideas which effect the education poilicy of the country. It depends on the concept of man and the values of life. In Indian philosophy moral and spiritual aspects of life are very important, it believed in practical type of things. The main viewpoint is that ignorance is the cause of suffering. Knowledge includes meditation on the accepted truths. It is a practical life of self control. Liberation cannot be achieved without sufficient knowledge of reality.

Objectives of the people have always been changing from time to time. In times ancient, they were influenced by the Vedas, the Upanishads, the Puranas etc. The relationship between philosophy and education was established during the Vedic period. Indian philosophers always say that there is need of education to know Satya (truth). Atma (Soul) and Brahma' (knowledge). They believe that education removes the ignorance of many. It helps the individual to attain the Absolute-Truth-Beauty, Goodness. The aim of education is liberation from the cycle of birth and death.

Indian Philosophy

Concept of Knowledge. 'Ved' means to know and the Vedas means the book of knowledge. The Vedas are regarded the soul of true knowledge. Outwardly there are four Vedas but they are all one and the same. Every Veda comprises of three part (i) Mantras (ii) Brahamanas (iii) Upnishads.

The Vedas show the infancy of Indian philosophy and religion. Here ma' considered the physical powers as the ultimate powers, in Upnishads, human thought had become more mature. No of the man said that natural powers were not the ultimate reality.

According to Upanishads, ultimate reality is Brahma—the infinite. Brahma is existence. Brahma is knowledge. Knowledge is obtained through the activity of mind. It is the product of reason. The Upanishads divide knowledge into two categories (i) para vidya (ii) apara vidya. They say that the world originates in Brahma, remains in Him and then goes into Him. Brahma is everywhere. Even today concept of education is the same in India. Education aims at - (i) preservation and transmission of culture (ii) development of personality (iii) and self-realization.

Concept of Reality or Truth. Brahma is the greatest truth in this world. It is perfect and is the only truth. It is the basis of all knowledge. The knowledge of Brahma is the eternal truth. The Upanishads emphasize again and again that truth is revealed step by step. The nature of Reality is 'spiritual' and 'mental'. The inner world is the real world. The outer world is one aspect of reality. It can be understood by meditation.

The origin of Bhagvad Gita is in the great epic Mahabharat. The Gita is the most influential work in Indian philosophy. The Geeta is the essence of the philosophy of Upanishads. It has contributed the Doctrine of Karam Yoga.

Through Nishkama Karam, a person understands the truth and realizes the self which leads to salvation.

The philosophy of Geeta says that education should help in the development of physical, mental, social and spiritual aspects of man's life. He should understand the ideals of life-Dharma Artha, Kama and Moksha. The philosophy of Geeta is that a person can understand the truth through his just activities. Education helps the individual to understand the reality.

Concept of Values. Indian philosophy believes that there are eternal values of life i.e. Truth, Beauty and Goodness. These are not confined to the physical level only. They belong to higher level of thinking. Idea of goodness is the supreme reality. Others derive their being from it. Education is given for the achievement of Universal values.

In ancient India, the philosophy of eduation was inspired by the following values:

Liberation of the individual. Evil arises out of ignorance. Ignorance is a limitation. Education helps to remove ignorance. Education is a means to attain freedom from ignorance.

Tolerance and Forbearance. Tolerance and forbearance were important. All individuals are the creations of Brahma. Brahma alone is real. Everything else is the manifestation of Brahma. So everything is worthy of respect and regard.

Disinterested Devotion (Nishkama Bhakti). Another value of Indian philosophy of education was 'Disinterested Devotion' (Nishkama Bhakti), Once the evils were overcome, the individual realised himself. Then he found himself with the Absolute.

Thus we find that education is an instrument through which the individual can rise higher. He can achieve the Absolute Truth, Beauty and Goodness. Education can help in social efficiency, develop character and cultivate spiritual vlaues.

Concept of Education

Man becomes a man through education. Man is what education makes him. Education makes a man a complete man. Education makes man a fit person for society- are significant guidelines which give an idea of what we mean by education. In the words of Willmatt, "Education is the apprenticeship of life.

The word 'education' is derived from two Latin words (i) Eduoare and (ii) Educere. 'Educar' means to bring up' or 'to nourish'. Naturally education then brings up the child in view of the aims and objectives. The Latin word 'educere' means to draw out or to lead out. Accordingly education through its process draws out of the best what is inside the child. In the words of Ross, "Education consists in leading out the innate knowledge, virtues and powers of the child, making the potential actual." :

Various views are mentioned below:

1. According to Rig Veda, "Education is something which makes a man self-reliant and selfless."
2. According to H.Mann, "A human being is not, if any proper sense, a human being till he is educated."
3. Addison says, "What sculpture is to block of marble, education is to the human soul. The philosopher, the saint, the wise and the good, or the great, very often lie hid and concealed in a plebeian, which a proper education might have discovered and brought to light."
4. O'Shea put forth the view, "Character development is the great if not the sole, aim of education."
5. In the words of Austin O'M "Education should be a conscious methodical application of the best means in the wisdom of the ages to the end that you may know how to live completely."
6. Daniel Webster says, "Knowledge does not comprise all which is contained in the large term of education. The

feelings are to be restrained; time and worthy motives are to be inspired; a profound religious feeling is to be instilled, and pure morality indicated under all circumstances. All this is comprised in education."

7. Here Nicholas Murray Butler's views are worth quoting. He says, "There are five tests of the evidence of eduation; correctness man and precision in the use of the mother tongue; refined and gentle manners, the result of fixed habits of thought and action; and a character based on those standards; power and habit of reflection; efficiency or the power to do."
8. According to Upanishads, "Education is that whose end-product is salvation."
9. According to Yajnavalkya. "Education is that which makes a man of good character and useful to the world."
10. The renowned Indian Statesman and lawgiver Kautilya says, "Education means training for the country and love for the nation."
11. According to Guru Nanak Dev Ji, "Education consists in service to others." He believed in reforming others.
12. Swami Vivekananda considered education as, "the manifestation of divine perfection already existing in man." He refers to the development of divine potential already ingrained in man.
13. According to Swami Dayanand, "Education is a means for character formation and righteous living."
14. According to Tagore. "Education is that which makes one's life in harmony with all existence and thus enables the mind to find out that ultimate truth which gives us the wealth of inner light and love and gives significance of life."
15. According to Dr. Zakir Hussain, "Education is the process of the individual mind getting to its full possible development."
16. The University Education Commission (1948-49) described education as "initiation into the life of spirit, a training of

human soul in the pursuit of truth and the practice of virtue. It is a second birth, "dvitiya janma."

17. According to the report of Indian Education Commission (1964-66), "Education ought to be related to the life, needs and aspirations of the people and thereby made powerful instrument of social, economic and cultural transformation."

18. T.P. Nunn says, "Education is the complete development of the individuality of the child so that he can make an original contribution to human life according to the best of his capacity."

19. According to Thompson, "Education is the influence of the environment on the individual with a view to producing a permanent change in his habits, behaviour, thought and attitude."

Thus, we find that education is a purposeful and deliberate effort:

1. to develop man in terms of his many sided personality.
2. to help him adjust to his environment.
3. to develop his body, mind and soul.
4. to develop his innate powers.
5. to help him become a real man.
6. to create a sound mind in a sound body.
7. to enable a person to have harmony with all existence.
8. to develop the mind of the individual to its fullest possible development.
9. to make a man of good character and useful to the world.
10. to help a person to have righteous living.

Relationship between Philosophy and Education

Philosophy and Education are inter-related and interdependent. Both go hand in hand with each other. They are means to one another and ends, they are process and product. Philosophy is the foundaton out of which comes the objectives of education.

According to Ross, "Philosophy and education are like the two sides of the same coin; the one is implied by the other ; the former is the contemplative side of life, while the latter is the active side."

John Dewey, "Education is the theory of education in its most general phase,'...."Education is a laboratory, in which philosphical distinctions, become concrete and are tested."

Spencer, "True education is practicable only to true philosophies."

Gentile, "Education without philosophy would mean a failure to understand the precise nature of education."

Connor's view, "Theory (Philosophy) directs practice (Education) and practice directs theory."

Philosophy determines the goals towards which education has to go. Thus philosophy determines wisdom to education transmits wisdom from one generation to the other.

Philosophy deals with the ends and education is the means to achieve those ends. Philosophy fixes up values, suggests ideal and lays down the principles. Education, in its process and through its means, tries to achieve them. So Herbert is right when he says: "Education has no time to make holiday till all the philosophical questions are once for all cleared up."

Philosophy is the contemplative side while education is its active side. The former deals with theoretical part and the latter with practical part thereof. It is doubtlessly right to say that education is the dynamic side of philosophy.

Great philosophers have also been great educationists. The great philosophers like Gandhi, Tagore, Ghosh, Radhakrishnan, Plato, Socrates, Locke, Confucius, Rousseau, Froebel and Dewey have been great educators. Their philosophical views and thoughts stand fully reflected in the educational schemes propagated by them. Socrates gave to the world the 'method of questioning and cross-questioning' in teaching. Rousseau suggested that education should follow nature, Gandhi propagated the scheme of Basic Education. Ross rightly said, "If further agreement is needed to establish the fundamental dependence of education on philosophy, it may be found that all great philosophers have been great educationists."

Philosophy is the basis of different aspects of education. If we see to aims, curriculum, textbooks, methods of teaching, class discipline, time table, teacher, headmaster we find that they are all determined by philosophy. Philosophy determines the aims of education and the aims determine the curriculum, the text books, the method of teaching, school discipline, role of the teacher and role of the headmaster.

Thus philosophy and education are inter-related and inter-dependent.

1. Philosophy is the foundation to decide the goals of life. Education then equals people suitably to achieve the said goal.
2. The different educational movements which have been prevalent in history of education were led by the great philosophers.
3. Philosophy determines what is worth living. Education then educates the man and prepares him for that type of life which is worth living.
4. Philosophy is the theoretical side, while education is the practical side. The former is contemplative whereas the latter is dynamic.
5. Philosophy indicates the values to be pursued in life. Education then inculcates those values in the learners.
6. Philosophy helps in clarifying the numerous eduational issues and problems.
7. Philosophy provides zeal and inspiration to the teachers and the Headmasters for accomplishing the educational tasks.

Impact on Different Aspects of Education

Every aspect of eduation has a philosophical base. It is philosophy which provides aims to education and these aims determine the curriculum, the methods of teaching and then decide the role of the teacher, pattern of discipline and so on.

Philosophy and Aims of Education. Education being a planned activity, has a number of aims. These aims are formulated by the philosophy of life. In the words of Bode, "Unless we have some guiding philosophy in the determination of objectives, we get nowhere at all."

In fact, philosophy formulates what should be the end of life and education, while education offers suggestions how this end is to be achieved.

Different philosophers of education describe different aims of education. Idealism, Naturalism and Pragmatism are three distinctive philosophies and each one of them recommends distinctive aims of education.

Idealism believes in self-enhancement, whereas naturalism prefers self-preservation. Pragmatism recommends socialisation of an individual. Similarly, aims of education have been different at different times and in different countries. Thus it is dear that aims of education are determined by philosophy. Ross rightly remarked, "The educational aims and methods are corollaries of philosophical doctrines."

Philosophy and Curriculum. Curriculum is the design of education. Through it, desired behavioural changes are sought to be achieved to attain the goals of life and education determined by a particular philosophy. It is philosophy which decides why a particular subject and activity should be included in the curriculum.

Brigffs has apply remarked, "It is just here that education seriously needs loader-leaders who hold sound comprehensive philosophy of which they can convince others and who can direct its consistent application to the formulation of appropriate curriculum.

Idealists emphasize higher values of life and prescribe the study of religion, ethics, literature and humanities.

Naturalists are mainly concerned with physical science and direct experiences.

Pragmatists Jay more stress on the study of functional subjects and social sciences.

So it is clear that philosophy is in the background of every type of curriculum.

Philosophy and Methods of Teaching

Philosophy is also closely, related to the methods of teaching. Philosophy is a way of thinking and a way of working. As such, these two factors determine the nature, style and actual operation of methods of teaching.

Kilpatrick's use the term "Philosophy of Methods" shows that there is a close relation between educational method and philosophy."

Every school of philosophy has its own methods of teaching. Idealism advocates question-answer method, lecture and discussion method. Naturalists recommend learning by doing. Heuristic method, self learning and direct experiences. Pragmatists recommended prefect method, socialised techniques, problem-solving method and the like.

Philosophy and Discipline. Philosophy also determines the nature and form of discipline. Whether school discipline should be strict and rigid or flexible and free is also a philosophical problem. It may be pointed out that social, political, economic and philosophical thinking of a particular country always determines the nature of discipline.

Modern concept of discipline is in tune with the principle of democracy and social philosophy.

Philosophy and the Teacher. Philosophy has great influence on the teacher both in the area of thinking and behaving. Every teacher is a philosopher. He influences the personality of the child and given him a new outlook of life. In this context Gentile remarked, "The belief that men may continue to educate without concerning themselves with philosophy means a failure to understand the precise nature of education. The process of education cannot go on right lines without the help of philosophy."

An idealist teacher is a man of higher ideals. He is indispensible. Naturalism accepts a teacher as a stage setter and working behind the scene. He is not to interfere in the education of the child in a direct way. According to Pragmatism, a teacher is a friend and guide facilitating the process of growth of an individual.

Philosophy also influences school practices and daily schedule. A school will reflect a particular philosophy in its organisational pattern. Similarly, philosophy has its edge over the textbooks, and the process of evaluation.

In each philosophy of educaton, there is a specific role of the teacher. Philosophy rather gives a sense of adventure to the teacher.

The Scope

By scope, we mean the area or the range within which it functions. That way, the scope of educational philosophy to unlimited because it deais with the schools of philosophy which are concerned with-education. Philosophy of education considers almost all the aspects of education. What sbould be the aims of education, what type of curriculum will be all right for the attainment of those goals.

The following points show clearly the scope of educational philosophy:

Aims of Education. Aims of education are determined with the help of educational philosophy. Without the help of educational philosophy, the teacher finds it difficult to reach or fix up rightly the goals of education which are suitable for the right growth and development of an individual. When there are no aims, any effort to work, any plan to materialise would remain a futile exercise.

Preparing the Curriculum. Aims of education lead to determine the type of curriculum which will be suitable for the learners. It is only educational philosophy which helps in deciding what contents will be all right and why those contents will be more suitable.

Realities behind Teaching Learning Programme. Educational philosophy can determine rightly about the nature of the learner, the nature of the society, the nature of the world, the nature of the school etc. Right answers to the different questions that crop up are possible only through the knowledge of educational philosophy.

The above mentioned points show very clearly that the scope of educational philosophy is unlimited. It has no ending. In this context, Plato says that a philospher gets pleasure in all kinds of knowledge and he is never satisfied with the knowledge that he acquires.

The Functions

1. Philosophy of education gives original thoughts on different aspects of education. Its main function is to consider the aims of education. Educational philosophy draws the attention of the teachers, the student, the authorities to the different aims of education. It is rather sad to know that these days everybody is more concerned with the means and less concerned with the ends. More improtance is given to the teaching methods, the management of the building, the arrangement of furniture etc. and less care is for the aims.

2. The overall function of educatonal philosophy is to answer all the fundamental questions of education.

3. Another important function of philosophy of education is the all round development of the personality of the learner. Here what are the different elements included in the all round development and which element should be given more importance-all these are rightly decided by philosophy of education.

According to Brubacher, the different functions of educational philosophy are as under:

(a) Speculative Function. One important function of philosophy of education is to speculate. That way, it "leads the educator and the educational administrator from common sense approach to rational and perspective approach." When facts, data, information etc. have been collected, educational philosophy makes assessment of everything. Thus it guides the teacher by giving him an overall view of the whole thing.

(b) Normative Function. The word 'normative' comes from the word norm. Philosophy sets the norms, goals, principles, standards etc. By applying these norms, we are able to decide things so as it reach the right decisions. In the absence of these norms, the teacher or the administrator or the controlling authorities fail to take the right decisions.

Prof. V.R. Taneja writes: "When man is faced with difficulties, strains and stresses, contradictory situations, unforeseen circumstances, and intriguing problems, philosophy enables him to consider the 'pros' and 'cons' and arrive at correct solution."

Philosophy combines with education and then its helps the teacher and the administrator to have clear vision of everything and that helps them attain their goals. Brubacher remarks that "Balance of mind and search for principles is the main spring of philosophy."

Critical Function. Dealing critically with different aspects of education is another important function of educational philosophy. That way, it examines the contents, the methodology in the sphere of education and refines it, modifies it to make it fully suitable.

John Dewey says: "Education is the laboratory in which philosophical distinctions become concrete and are tested."

Conclusion

Thus we find that philosophy effects different aspects of education. In the absence of philosophical foundations, education becomes irrelevant, meaningless and lifeless. Rusk has rightly said, "From every angle of educational problem comes thus the demand of a philosphical basis of the subject." There is no escape from a philosophy of life and of education. In short, philosophy leads and education follows the path shown uy philosophy. Butler says, "Philosophy is a guide to educational practice, education as field of investigation yields certain data as a basis for philosophical judgement." The need of the hour is to synthesise the different aspects and have a suitable philosophy of education. The effect of science and technology should also be realized fully. In this regard, Education Commission Report (1964-66) says, "in the developments that we envisage our future we hope that the pursuit of mere material affluence and power would be subordinated to that of higher values and the fulfilment of the individual. This concept of mingling of 'science and spirituality' is of special significance for Indian Education."

Assignments

How are philosophy and education related to each other? Write by giving suitable examples.

"All educational questions are ultimately the questions of philosophy." Discuss by giving examples from Indian background.

"Philosophy being a living and dynamic force influences education at all levels." Discuss.

"Education is the dynamic side of philosophy." Discuss in your own words.

What is the relation between Education and Philosophy? Why should every teacher make a study of philosophy?

Justify the need for the study of philosophy of education. Illustrate how it influences objectives of education and methods of teaching.

"Philosophy and Education are two sides of the same coin." Discuss.

"Education without philosophy is blind and philosophy without education is invalid." Discuss.

"Education is the practical aspect of philosophy and philosophy is intellectual aspect of education." Do you agree with this statement? Discuss fully by giving suitable arguments.

4

Major Philosophies

Philosophy and Human life exist together. Wherever human life exists, it has its philosophical bases which make life worth living. So one philosophy of education or the other always exists there. A few important philosophies of education are: Idealism ; Naturalism ; Pragmatism ; Progressivism ; Marxism ; Existentialism ; Materialism ; Spiritualism. Let us discuss a few of the philosophies.

Idealism

According to Oxford Dictionary, "Idealism means representation of things in an ideal form, imaginative treatment, system of thought in which the object of external perception is held to consist of ideas." in literature, the word "idealism" is used in literary sense. In philosophy, it mostly relates to 'idea.'

Idealism is a very old philosophical thought. Its inception is taken from the very times when man began to think. In West, it was born out of the writings and orations of Plato, Socrates and Aristotle. In India, it was born out of the scripts of Vedas, Puranas, Upanishads. Since then it has been growing and developing.

It has greatly influenced man and his mind. Even today it has its appeal to many. It has diverted the attention of great philosophies of the world. Those who advocated this philosophy were Socrates, Plato, Kant, Hegel, Berkley, Comenius, Froebel, Fichte, the Vedic, Rishis, Guru Nanak, Swami Vivekananda, Swami Dayanand, Ravindra Nath Tagore, Mahatma Gandhi and Radhakrishnan.

The word 'idealism' has been derived from the 'ideal' and 'idea'. The main subject of this philosophy is 'idea', the reality of every thing lies in ideas, thoughts and mind and not in material things. Ideas or higher values are essence, they are of ultimate cosmic significance. Nature is only an 'appearance' whereas mind is the 'reality'. Idealism believes in the supernatural reality.

Philosophical Meaning. Idealism seeks to offer an explanation of the man and the universe in terms of spirit of mind. Idealism is, in fact, spiritualism. Man's spiritual nature is considered to be the very essence of his being. It asserts that reality is to be found in man's mind rather than in material nature.

D.M. Dutta puts forth the view, "Idealistic philosophy takes many and varied forms, but the postulate underlying all this is that mind or spirit is the essential world stuff, that the true reality is of a mental character."

Rusk says, "Idealism contends that the material and physical universe known to science is an incomplete expression of reality, that it exists but to subserve and requires to complement it a higher type of reality, a spiritual universe."

According to Brubacher, "Idealists point out that it is mind that is central in understanding the world. To them nothing gives a greater sense of reality than the activity of mind engaged in trying to comprehend its world. For anything to give a greater sense of reality would be a contradiction in terms because to know anything more real than mind would itself be a conception of mind."

Basic Principles

Spirit and Mind constitute Reality. Idealism believes that spiritual nature of man is the essence of his being. The mental or spiritual is more real and important than material.

Man being Spiritual is a Supreme Creation. According to idealism, the supreme aim of life is "exaltation of human personality." Man is a spiritual being and it distinguishes him from other animals. Reality is found in the mind of man. Ross says, "Human personality is of supreme value and constitutes the noblest work of God."

Universal Mind. Idealism believes in the Universal Mind. Our little mind is a part of it. The goal of human life is to realise the Universal Mind. H.N. Home remarked, "An idealistic philosophy of education, then, is an account of man finding himself as an integral part of universal mind."

Faith in Spiritual Values. According to idealism, Values are absolute and unchanging. The prime aim of human life is to achieve spiritual values. These are Truth, Beauty and Goodnes. These values are absolute, permanent. In the pursuit of these values, man uses higher and higher till he attains Divinity. Ross opines, "Goodness, Truth and Beauty are seen to be absolutes each existing in its own right and entirely desirable in self."

Real knowledge is perceived in Mind. God is the source of all knowledge. Knowledge through the activity, creativity and exercise of the mind is more important than the knowledge acquired through sense .

Idealism in Education

The credit of introducing idealism in education goes to Plato. Education according to idealism, is a spiritual necessity and not a natural necessity. Idealists believe that man's nature is spiritual and divine. He can realise this through education.

Idealism and Aims of Education

Idealism prescribes certain fundamental aims of education which are directly influenced by the aims and principles of life. In this context Ross puts forth the view, "The function of education is to help us in our exploration of the ultimate universal values so that truth of the universe may become our truth and give power to our life." Some of the important aims of education as laid down by idealists are given below:

Self realisation. According to idealism, man is the most beautiful creation of God-His grandest work. It lays great stress on the exaltation of human personality. It is self-realisation. The aim of education is to develop the 'self of the 'individual's higher till self-realisation is achieved. It is, in fact, making actual or real the highest potentialities of the self.

Universal Education. Education according to idealism, should be universal in nature. The universe is regarded as a thought process. Education should be based on the teaching of universal truth from the stand-point of rationality of the universe.

Spiritual Development. Idealists give greater importance to spiritual values in comparison with material attainments. According to Rusk', "Education must enable mankind through its culture to enter more and more fully into the spiritual realm, and also enlarge the boundaries of spiritual realm."

Transmission and Promotion of Cultural Heritage. The aim of idealistic education is the preservation, enrichment and transmission of culture. Education must contribute to development of culture. It should help in enlarging the boundaries of spiritual realm. The child has to be introduced to his cultural heritage so as to enable him to conserve, promote and transmit it to rising generation.

Cultivation of Moral Values. According to idealism, man is essentially a moral being. Therefore, moral, intellectual and aesthetic aspects of his personality should be promoted. According to Dr. Prem Nath, "The process of education must lead to the deepest spiritual insight and to the highest moral and spiritual conduct.

Preparation for a Holy Life. Idealism prepares an individual for a holy life. Froebel says, "The object of education is the realization of a faithful, pure, inviolable and hence holy life."

Development of intelligence and Rationality. Idealism wishes that education should develop the mind fully. It makes a person rational as well. Only the highly developed mind can understand the all pervading force. Froebel says, in his book 'Education of Man': "in all things there reigns an eternal law.......... this all pervading energetic, self-conscious and hence eternal unity. This unity is God. Education should lead and guide man to face nature and to unify with God. Dr. Prem Nath says, "The process of education must lead to the deepest spiritual insight and to the highest moral and spiritual conduct."

In short, the idealists believe that education must help in the full evolution of mind, the emancipation of spirit, self-realisation and the realisation of higher values of life and to train "the whole man completely and fully for manhood and not some part of man."

Idealism and Curriculum

While developing curriculum, idealists give more importance to thought, feelings, ideals and values than to the child and his activities. They firmly hold that curriculum should be concerned with the whole humanity and its experiences. It must consist of humanities.

The curriculum should give good mental experience of all types. So cognition (knowing), affecting (feeling), and conation (striving) should find due place. Sciences and arts should be taught as fully integrated. Since the main aim of education according to the philosophy of idealism is to preserve and advance the culture of human race, so subjects like Religion, Ethics, Philosophy, History, Literature etc. should be provided in the curriculum. Healthy mind is found in healthy body only. So health, hygiene, games and sports should find an important place in the curriculum. For intellectual development, subjects like Languages, Science, Mathematics etc. should be there.

According to Rusk, the idealist's curriculum may be represented as:

Care of body	Physical Skills	Activities Education
Intellectual Spiritual	Moral Activities	Aesthetic Religious

Idealism and Methods of Teaching

Idealism has not prescribed specific methods of teaching. According to idealism, class-room is a temple of spiritual teaming, a meeting place of human minds-a place for self education. For this no particular method has been suggested. However, the following methods have been advocated by different idealists:

1. Learning through reading.
2. Learning through lecturing.
3. Learning through discussion.
4. Learning through imitation.
5. Learning through questioning.
6. Descrates employed the device of simple to complex.

Herbert advocated instruction method, while Froebel insisted upon Play way method. In all, Socrates Method and Discussion Method form the basis of idealism. Butler rightly remarked, "Idealists consider themselves as creators and determiners of methods not devotees of some one method."

Idealism and Discipline

Naturalism provides unrestricted freedom to the child whereas Idealism wants to keep the child under discipline. Idealists believe that there can be no spiritual development of the child without discipline. This leads to inner discipline. "The discipline is not to be imposed on pupils. The teacher has only to help them to develop self-discipline and through that self-knowledge."

Self-insight and self analysis are the main disciplinary factors. The main task of education is the cultivation of higher values of life through moral and religious education. It requires the teacher to present a good example and exercise lasting impact upon the pupil's mind. A teacher is an ideal person to be emulated by his pupils

Idealism and the Teacher

Idealism assigns a special role to the teacher. It considers teacher as a spiritual guide for the child. The teacher serves as a living model for the students. He sets the environment in which education takes place. He carries the child from darkness to light. He is to guide the student towards utmost possible perfection.

Idealism regards the teacher as the priest of man's spiritual heritage. He is a co-worker wtth God in perfecting man. An idealist teacher is a philosopher, friend and guide. According to Gentite-A teacher is "a spiritual symbol of right conduct." He is thus, an indispensable necessity.

According to Ross, 'in the idealistic scheme of studies, the teacher is needed to assist the educated who is developing according to the laws of nature, to attain levels that would otherwise be denied to him."

The teacher is to be an ideal person-personification of reality. He is to be a source of inspiration for the students. So he should embody the spiritual qualities of mankind.

According to Froebd, the school is a garden, the teacher is a cautious gardener and the child is a tender plant. The plant can grow, no doubt, without help but the good gardener sees that the plant grows to the finest possible perfection. Through teacher's guidance the child can make his natural development tnto a process leading to perfection and beauty. Ross explains, "The naturalist may be patient but the idealist wants fine roses."

Thus we find that the philosophy of idealism has contributed richly to the field of education. But this does not mean it has no shortcomings. It has a few drawback which are enlisted below:

Shortcomings of Idealism

1. Idealism may be considered to be outmoded in the prevailing scientific world view.
2. Idealistic concepts like 'spirit', 'mind', 'soul', and the cosmos' have little relevance in the class-room teaching.
3. There is too much emphasis on good manners and modesty which may be mistaken.
4. It neglects child's psychological nature.
5. Idealism does not contribute to methods of teaching.
6. It sets unobtainable goals.
7. Idealistic scheme of education, by and large, pays attention to physical, industrial, social and electronic environment of today.
8. It neglects social aspects of life.
9. It over emphasizes humanity and under rates science and technology.

In all, we can say that idealistic approach to education has its own merits and shortcomings. It should, therefore, be supplemented by other philosophy or philosophies of education.

Naturalism

Idealism, Naturalism and Pragmatism are three schools of philosophy which have influenced education most in theory as well as practice. Naturalism is comparatively modern.

The naturalistic movement headed by Jean Jacques Rousseau was a revolution in thought and practice. Naturalism may be regarded as a revolt against the stereotyped system of education. It is reaction against artificiality of life. Nature is the ultimate reality and it is a self-sufficient entity. According to the naturalists only the natural world is the real world. "Nature alone contains the normal and the final answers to all philosophical problems." Back to nature is the watch word of naturalism. Naturalism believes that reality and nature are identical and that beyond nature, there is no reality. Naturalism does not believe in sentimentalism, spiritualism and supernaturalism.

Definitions

1. Adams, View, "Naturalism is a term loosely applied in educational theory to systems of training that are not dependent on schools and books but on the manipulation of the actual life of the educated."
2. Ward's View, "Naturalism is the doctrine which separates nature from God, subordinates spirit of matter and sets up unchangeable laws as supreme."
3. Dr. Prem Nath's View, "Naturalism is an attitude rather than a specific system of philosophy."
4. Hocking's View. "Naturalism is metaphysics which considers nature as the whole of reality. It excludes what is supernatural or other world."
5. Rusk's View, "Naturalism is a philosophical position adopted by those who approach philosophy from purely scientific point of view."
6. R.B. Perry's View, "Naturalism is the philosophical generalization of sdence-the application of the theories of science to the problems of philosophy."'

In the words of Ross, "Naturalism is a term loosely applied in educational theory to systems of training that are not dependent on schools or books but on the manipulation of the actual life of the educated."

Democritus, Bacon, Comenius, Herbert Spencer, Hux, Rousseau, Pestalozzi, Tagore, T.P. Nunn are some of the chief exponents of Naturalism.

Characteristics

Nature alone is the entire Reality. Both nature and reality are identical. Hocking writes, "Naturalism denies existence of anything beyond nature, behind nature, other than nature, such as the supernatural or other wordly."

Laws of Nature. Laws of nature are superb and they are unchangeable. Everything in this universe is governed by them.

Mysteries of Nature. Mysteries of nature are revealed through scientific methods.

Senses-the Gate Way. Senses are the natural gate ways to knowledge. All knowledge is comprehensible through senses.

The Universe is all Material in Character. The whole universe is made purely of matter. There is no soul or spirit in it. Everything is governed by laws of physical sciences. Matter alone constitutes the universe.

Society is only an Artificial Structure. Man creates societies only to meet some of his needs. The individuals alone are real.

Scientific Knowledge. According to the naturalists, scientific knowledge is of the highest worth. Science is the source of all knowledge.

Nature has History. Nature has a history of its own. It grows and evolves with the passage of time. Man also is changed with the lapse of time.

Schools of Naturalism

The following are the three forms of Naturalism:

1. Physical Naturalism.
2. Mechanical Naturalism.
3. Biological Naturalism.

Physical Naturalism. Physical naturalism studies the process of matter and phenomena of the external world. It explains human activities and experiences in terms of material objects and natural laws. In other words, Physical Naturalism lays more stress on the external material phenomena than the conscious human being. In fact, reality is visualised as physical substance.

Mechanical Naturalism. According to mechanical naturalism this universe is a lifeless huge machine which gets its form through matter and motion. Man is considered as a mere part of huge machine and is himself a small machine. This machine is run by time guiding principles and these principles are natural. This form of naturalism has given rise to modern psychology of behaviouralism.

Biological Naturalism. This form of naturalism is based on the theory of evolution put forth by Darwin. According to this, man has evolved from lower animals by a gradual process of evolution. Biological naturalism emphasises the development of man's natural impulses, natural propensities and inborn tendencies. The doctorine has put forward three principles of evolution such as:

1. Adaptation to Environment.
2. Struggle for Existence.
3. Survival of the Fittest.

Naturalism in Education

Like all other philosophies, Naturalism exerted a great influence on the theory as well as practice of education. In the naturalistic system of education, there is no place for class-rooms, textbooks, time-table and formal examinations. The chalk and talk method has no scope here. There is discipline of natural consequences. Thus naturalism is only a negative philosophy as it stands against the prevailing system of teaching.

Revolt against the Traditional System of Education. Naturalism may be regarded as a revolt against the traditional system of education. It is against bookish knowledge, it believes that education should be in strict conformity with the nature of the child. It encourages, formulates and applies natural laws to the educative process.

Child as the Centre of All Education. Naturalism advocates the reorganisation of education in such a way that all shackles of formalism, verbosity etc. are broken and the development of the child goes on according to his inherent nature, needs and inborn propensities.

'Follow Nature' is the slogan for effective education. Rousseau, the champion of Naturalism declared that all bonds of artificiality should be broken down and education should be given according to the natural interests and and tendencies of the child so that he develops his personality fully and completely.

Emphasis on Freedom. Naturalism gives prominent place to the concept of freedom in the education of the child. The child would be given freedom to live in a nature without any type of checks and controls. Thus his whole learning will come from his own experiences and their natural consequences.

Naturalists Advocate Co-education. According to them, it is unnatural to separate the two sexes.

The entire education of the child should be based on his inborn tendencies, impulses and emotions.

Unncessary burden of educational instructions be avoided. Let education generate happiness and good mood.

In short, Naturalism is a sort of revolution against the traditional aims, ideals, curriculum and methods of teaching. Both Rousseau and Herbert Spencer put the child at the central position of educational process. Thus child-centred and scientific tendency in education are the two important aspects of Naturalism in education.

Naturalism and Aims of Education

The main aims of education as advocated by Naturalism are as under:

Self-Expression. Idealism gives importance to self-realisation, whereas the main aim of naturalism is self-expression and self-preservation.

Perfection of Human Machine. In the words of Ross, "Education should make the human machine as good a machine as possible by attending to its constitution, by elaborating it and making it capable of more and more complicated tasks."

Re-direction and Human instincts. Me Dougall regards the instincts of man as the prime movers of his behaviour. Education should, therefore, aim at the re-direction and sublimation of these instincts.

Struggle for Existence. The evolutionists consider education to equip the individual for struggle of his existence and thus to ensure his survival.

Education for Adjustment. Education also aims at helping the individual to secure his adjustment-physical as well as mental. Educations regarded as the process of adjustment to environment.

Autonomous Development of Individuality. The aim of Naturalistic education is to ensure complete development of individuality without any interference by the society. Rousseau and T.P. Nunn are the champions of this view. Individuality is the ideal of life.

Improvement of Racial Gains. Bernard Shaw remarks that alongwith the transmission of physical traits, racial experience should also be transmitted. Education fulfils this responsibility.

Education According to the Nature of the Child. It has been rightly said that, "Education finds its purpose, its process and its means within the child-life and child-experience." Nature of the child should be first understood for this purpose.

According to H. Spencer, "The aim of education is to enable the pupil to achieve his present and future happiness by cultivating in him the habit of self-restraint and a sense of proper values."

According to Darwin the exponent of the Theory of Evolution, "The only function of education is to equip the individual for facing the struggle for existence and ensure his survival in it."

In this regard Me Dougall says, "Education is intended to sublimate the child's instincts and humanise his natural impulses and thus enable him to reach his natural goals."

In all, education should develop the child into Joyous, rational, harmoniously balanced, useful and mature child.

Naturalism and Curriculum

Naturalism does not advocate any rigid or fixed curriculum. Its firm belief is that child teams best in natural settings:

1. It is based on the psychology of the child. Naturalistic curriculum is based on the nature of the child, his interests and inborn tendencies.
2. It lays stress on subjects that are helpful in self-preservation. Spencer contends that only those subjects should be included in the curriculum which help in self-preservation.
3. It stresses basic sciences. Naturalists lay emphasis on science subjects such as Physics, Chemistry, Biology, Arithmetic, Zoology, Botany etc. Language, Literature, Art etc. are subsidiary subjects.
4. It emphasises physical and health education.
5. It lays stress on the study of past experiences of the race. The past experiences explain the origin of the present ones. Therefore, subjects like history, geography should also be included in the curriculum.
6. There is no place for religious and moral education. Such education is a matter of experiences rather than of instruction. Punishment is given by nature in its own way.

Naturalism and Methods of Teaching

In the field of methodology, Naturalism has made very significant contribution. It discards all rigid, uniform and traditional techniques of teaching. Teaching in class-rooms does not find favour with the naturalists. Here the exmphasis is on the individual method. Rousseau says, "Give your scholar no verbal lesson, he should be taught by experience alone."

Naturalism lays stress on:

1. Learning by doing. It is based on the principles of child activity and participation.
2. Learning through experience. Naturalism believes in self-education. Child learns through his personal experiences with things and nature. So he should be encouraged to discover things for himself.
3. Learning through observation. Naturalism believes in self-education. Child learns through his personal experiences with things and nature. So he should be encouraged to discover things for himself.
4. Learning through observation. Science should be taught through observation and experimentation.
5. Heuristic method. Naturalism advocated Heuristic method for teaching Science and Mathematics because that way the child is placed in the situation of self-discoverer.

Other methods of teaching recommended by Naturalism are play way method, Dalton Plan, Direct study of natural phenomena and Experimentation.

Naturalism and Discipline

Naturalism gives full freedom to the child for self-expansion. Human nature is essentially good and pure. Therefore, no external discipline is desirable. Adults' standards must not be forced upon the children. Discipline by natural consequences. Naturalism believes in discipline by natural consequences. Nature gives the consequence of activity in the form of pleasure or pain

Spencer says, "when a child falls or runs its head against the table, it suffers pain, the rememberance of which tends to make it more careful and by repetition of such experiences, it is disciplined into proper guidance of its movement." He, however, gives a line of caution by saying, "A three year old child playing with an open razor cannot be allowed to go by this discipline for the consequences may be too serious." John Oewey does not agree with this view and prefer warning showing disfavour etc.

In short, Naturalists decry all kinds of external interference, repressionistic measures and allow full freedom to the child with emphasis on respect for child's personality.

Naturalism and Teacher

Nature is a great teacher. Naturalists consider Nature as the only supreme teacher in whose close contact the child develops normally and naturally. Naturalists do not like that children should be taught in classes by teachers. In the .naturalistic scheme of education the teacher plays the rote of an observer. His job is to facilitate the process of child's growth as well as teaming. Rosa says that "The teacher is only a setter of the stage, a supplier of materials and opportunities, a provider of an ideal environment, a creator of conditions under which natural development takes place."

The teacher is only a means to assist child's full and free development.

Drawbacks of Naturalism

Naturalism suffers from a few drawbacks which are briefly given below:

1. Naturalism ignores the spiritual and moral sides of man's nature.
2. It attends to only the present needs of the child and ignores his future needs. The ultimate ideals and purposes of man's life are not cared for.
3. Naturalism in its extreme form neglects books and other media.
4. Physical nature alone is not sufficient for providing education.
5. It is based on one-sided psychology.
6. Absolute freedom to the child is rather impossible.

7 It regards human beings as more of an animal being.

8. Direct experience cannot be provided all the time.

9. Naturalism assigns very little importance to the teacher in the educative process.

Good and bad points are always there. On the whole, its contribution is unique. It has effected modern methods of teaching considerably. It has made teaching real and'useful.

Pragmatism

Pragmatism stands for progessive treads in education. It is midway between Naturalism and Idealism, it is an American philosophy typical in nature and practical in approach. Between theory and practice, pragmatism states that practice comes first and theory afterwards. Pragmatism is twentieth century revolution against 19th century rationalism, dogmatism and universalism. The chief exponents of this philosophy are-WIlliam James. C'harles S. Pierce, John Dewey, W.H Kilpatrick. Margret H. Mead etc.

According to James, the term "pragmatism" is derived from the Greek word 'pragma' which means action, turned as words 'practice' and 'practical' have been derived. To James there is no difference between pragmatism and practicalism.

James. B. Prett says, "Pragmatism offers us a theory of meaning, a theory of truth of knowledge, and a theory of reatity."

In the words of J.S. Ross, 'Pragmatism is essentially a humanistic philosophy, maintaining that man creates his own values in the course of activity, that reality is still in the making and awaits its part of completion from the future, that to an unascertainable extent our truths are man-made products."

Thus great importance is given to practice and utility. Action gets priority over thought. Experience is at the centre of the universe. Pragmatism is also known as Experimentalism or Consequentialism. Pragmatism sees thought as intrinsically connected with action. The value of an idea is measured by the consequences produced when it is translated into action. Thus pragmatism is an attitude, a method and a philosophy.

Pramatism believes that philosophy is not a wisdom of the past. True-philosophy is that which helps in solving the problems of life. John Oswey says, "Philosophy, in order to be philosophy, should have meaning and utility in Influencing the conduct of life and not a passive enquiry or contemplation." According to Pragmatism, 'Philosophy is thinking what to do in a life situation and it is brought into existence when problems occur".

Professor Arnold Raid regards pragmatism as 'activity', 'engagement', 'encounter'. Pragmatism is based on the concept of practice, or workability of an idea or theory. It further believes that, 'man is primarily an active, growing, animated, mobile who must first live life and only secondly speculate it."

Forms of Pragmatism

Humanistic Pragmatism. Truth is that which best satisfies human nature and welfare as a whole. Whatever fulfils man's purposes, desires and develops his life, is true.

Experimental Pragmatism. Truth is that which can be experimentally verified or whatever works.

Biological Pragmatism. It stresses the human ability of adaptation to the environment and that of adapting the environment to human needs.

Principles of Pragmatism

Changing Nature of Truth. Pragmatists do not believe in pre-determined truths. According to them, truth always changes. A certain thing was true to a person yesterday, may fail today and it may not remain the same for tomorrow truth is that which works and fulfils man's purpose! 'Truth is made just as health, wealth and strength are made in the course of expenence.' ln short, truth is not absolute or predetermined for all times to come.

Rejects Ultimate Values. Pragmatism does not believe in the ultimate or absolute values of life. Values are not fixed or predetermined. They are instrumental only. They are used as means to attain certain ends. Values emerge only in individual social situations. They are man made.

Thought is Subordinate to Action. Pragmatism gives supreme position to action. Activity is more important than the ideas. Ideas are born out of activities. In other words, thought is hand-maid of action.

Faith in Experimentation. According to pragmatism, human life is like a laboratory wherein each individual undertakes various experiments to solve the problems of his life.

Faith in Present and Immediate Future. Pragmatism does not stick to the past. Each individual has to solve the problems of his present and future life. Hence the present and the immediate future are of great value to him. The past is dead and gone.

Reality still in the Making. For pragmatism reality is not ready-made. It is still in the making. William James says, "For Naturalism, reality is ready-made and complete from all entirely, while for pragmatism it is still in making and awaits its parts of completion from the future."

Faith in Flexbility. According to pragmatism, nothing is fixed and final in the world. The world is in the state of flux and changing. Everything is in the process of change. Human life is also changing.

Faith in Humanism. Pragmatism is based on the concept of human values. It located and identifies values in the human experience.

Faith in Democracy. Pragmatism has its deep faith in democracy and social values. Democracy is a way of life. Man is a social being. Life, education and democratic process are all rolled into one.

Principle of Utility. Pragmatism is a utilisation ideology which holds that the reality of a principle lies in its utility. Only those ideas and things are true which have a utility for man.

Pragmatism in Education

Pragmatism is closely related to modern education. It stands for progressive trends in education. Activity lies at the centre of all educative process. Pragmatism approaches the problems of education from the pregressivist's viewpoint. "Progressives change. Change further implies novelty." So education cannot be conceived of as acquired once for all.

Education is not to follow any established philosophy. It the philosophy that has to follow educational practices. In other words, philosophy is the product of educational practice. Dewey describes philosophy "as the theory of education in its most general phase."

Characterisitics of Pragmatic Education

Education is a social necessity. It is a means by which society renews itself.

Progressive education. Pragmatic education is progressive in nature. It is flexible and changes with the changing circumstances of life.

Freedom and worth of the individual. It stands for freedom and worth of the individual personality. It works on the principles of democracy.

Education is a continuous process. Educational process has no end. It is a means as well as end. Edocatten means more education.

Education not Dynamic Side of Philosophy. Pragmatism does'not believe that education is the dynamic side of philosophy. It rather regards philosophy as the outcome of educational experiments. Philosophy is the product of philosophy.

Pragmatism and Aims of Education

Pragmatists do not believe in any preconceived aims of education. Aims are not fixed, immutable or final. They arise out of the on-going experience and should be wholly within the child's experience. Some of the aims suggested in pragmatism are given below:

The Aim of Education is More Education. Education leads to more education. Every learning experience results into more experience and is means of new learning.

All Round Development of an Individual. The aim of educational development of human personality is in terms of his physical, intellectual, social and moral aspects. Thus the essential aim of eaucation is to direct the impulses, interests and abilities towards the satisfaction of the felt needs of the child in his environment.

Continuous reconstruction of Experience. Education is a process of living through continuous reconstruction of experiences. Learning takes place through experiences transmitted as well as shared.

Social Efficiency. Another aim of education is to produce socially efficient persons. It is in fact socialisation of an individual. Social efficiency includes economic and cultural efficiency.

Continuous Growth. The aim of pragmatic education is to enable an individual to grow continuously. This growth takes place through mutual interactions end changing social order.

Personal Social Adjustment. The most important aim of edu. ation according to pragmatism is the problem of adjustment. The' individual has not only to adjust himself, but also to improve upon it. He must also cope with life situations and problems.

Pragmatism and Curriculum

Curriculum in the pragmatic scheme of education is broad based, diversified and flexible. It is developed on the basis of the following principles:

Principles of Utility. According to this principle, only those subjects, activities and experiences be included in the curriculum which are useful for the present needs of the child and also for the future requirements.

In the over-all plan of curriculum, subjects like Languages, Physical training, Geography, History, Agriculture, Home science for girls, sciences, social science, vocational and technical education, mathematics for boys should find proper place.

Principles of Child's Natural Interests. Curriculum should be based on the interests, aptitude and tastes of the child. It should be constructed with due regard to the stages of development of children. At the primary stages, it should include reading, writing, counting art, craft, natural science etc.

Principles of Experience. The third principle is child's activity, vocation and experience. The curriculum should consist of such varieties of learning experiences which promote original thinking and freedom to develop social and purposeful attitudes.

Principle of Integration. This principle deals with the integration of subjects and activities. Pragmatism regards knowledge as one unit. It cannot be divided into watertight compartments. Teaching of various units should be closely interlinked and correlated so as to form right concepts and proper understanding in children.

Thus pragmatic curriculum is dynamic, flexible and integrated which is related to the realities of life.

Pragmatism and Methods of Teaching

Pragmatism has contributed greatly in the field of methods of teaching. Methods of teaching should not be fixed. Methods must be useful and related to the interest of the child.They must involve practical work activities and productive experiences. Pragmatism lays emphasis on the following principles:

Principles of Purposive Process of Learning. Pragmatism opposes bookish knowledge and condemns those methods which are not useful and relevant to the problems and challenges of modem life. Methods of teaching should provide purposeful and practical experiences and activities.

Prinicple of Learning by Doing. According to this principle education should be imparted through activities and practical experiences. Pragmatism believes in action and actual participation of the child in life situations. This principle stresses the fact that a child should be put into real situations and problems of life and should be enabled to study the situations intelligently and to solve them absolutely. The child gains insight and capacities to face and solve the problems of life.

Principles of Integration. This principle lays stress on correlated teaching of all subjects. It seeks to maintain unity in diversity. The subjects, activities and experience should be integrated properly.

On the basis of these principles of pragmatism John Dewey and others developed Project Method. Kilpatrick defines a project as "a whole hearted purposeful activity proceeding in a social environment."

Through this method, a problem is posed and a situation is created. The problem requires reasoning, imagining, calculating, evaluating and judging. It is a meaningful activity. The pupils find a solution. It is carried to completion.

Another significant contribution of pragmatism is Experimental Method which holds that knowledge is gained after experimentation.

Pragmatism and Discipline

Pragmatism condemns enforced and strict discipline. It advocates social discipline based on child's interests, activities and a sense of responsibility.

In order to maintain this attitude socialised activities are essential. It is social discipline through and through. An induvidual cultivates moral and social values while living in the society. He shares responsibilities and imbibes virtues like toleration, mutual respect, respect for humanity and moral obligation towards self and others.

School should, therefore, provide situations and experiences for inner and self discipline. A child will thus become a true citizen in the real sense of the term.

Pragmatism and Teacher

In a pragmatic system of education, a teacher occupies an important position. He has to be active, alert and resourceful. He must be trained, efficient and a man of foresight. He has to create learning situations for the child. In different situations he remains a friend and helper.

Dr. Prem Nath has rightly remarked, "Child's personality is not be overshadowed by that of the teacher. The teacher is a friend and helper; he is to provide the child with opportunities for experimenting in the school and on the field."

Naturalism does not allow the teacher to interfere in the education of the child. Idealism makes the teacher indispensable. In pragmatism, a teacher adopts 'hand off' policy. The teacher is a man of superior wisdom, a senior partner and a sincere guide. Pragmatism puts heavy demands on the teacher.

Limitations

The philosophy of pragmatism has been criticised on account of the following limitations:

1. It does not raise the question of ultimate realty behind things. According to it, whatever is apparent is real. There is no place for spirit or essence.
2. Humanities and cultural activities find no place in the pragmatic scheme of education.

3. It ignores the past as well as the experiences of the past. It lays emphasis on the present and the future.
4. It does not provide regular and systematic instructions.
5. It is less practicable in the Indian schools.
6. The curriculum in pragmatism is haphazard. It is difficult to include all the basic skills and knowledge required by the learners.
7. It does not give fixed ideals of education. Such an education does not help much.

Inspite of these limitations, pragmatism has contributed tremendously. It is an attitude and a way of living which inspires the individual to look ahead and create new values for leading a better, a happier and a richer life. Therefore, its contributions to educational thought and practice cannot be overlooked.

Existentialism

Existentialism is the youngest philosophy. It represents a revolt against many outlooks and methods of traditional western philosophy. It is very difficult to find its roots in any of the ancient philosophies. It may be described as a modern twentieth century philosophy, which is primarily built upon the work of the contemporary scholars.

Existentialism is concerned with the actual human existence and the realisation of his essential freedom. Existentialism considers individuality as supreme. Society is a means of its development.

Its chief exponents are:

1. Soren Kierkeguam, the Danish philosopher.
2. Jean Paul Sarter, a French writer.
3. Kari Jaspers, a German philosopher.
4. Paul T'llich, and
5. Reinhold Niebuhr, the two leading protestant theologians.

Meaning of Existentialism

1. This has defined Existentialism "as an attitude that emphasizes human existence-that is the distinctive qualities

of individual persons-rather than man in the abstract or nature and the world in general."

Man's fundamental drive is the urge to exist and to the recognised as an individual.

2. Femando says, "Existentialism is a type of philosophy which endeavours to analyse the basic structures of human existence and calls individuals to an awareness of their existence in its essential freedom."

Existentialism rejects universal and abstract problem and dwells upon subjective awareness.

Existentialism is an attempt to reach the inmost core of human existence in a concrete and individual fashion.

Finally we can say that existentialism is essentially the philosophy of man and his attempt to reaffirm and regain the lost status of man in this advanced technological and mechanised society. Man is everything" is the watchword of existentialism.

Basic Assumptions/Fundamentalis of Existentialism

Existence precedes essence. Man discovered himself. His existence came first and he is now in the process of determining his essence. Man first is, then he defines himself. Sartre explains this concept, "What is meant by saying that existence precedes essence? It means that, it turns up, appears In the scene, and only afterwards defines himself. A person lives before he dies. Before death, a person can change his essence by doing good deeds and then he will die a noble death, defines himself. Individual alone creates values.

Man has no Prior Nature. There is no such thing as pre-existence of human nature. There was nothing before birth end would be nothing beyond death. Original human nature is empty. It is acquired rather than inherited.

Value of Human Personality. Every human individual is unique. Man is the centre of the universe and nothing is equal to it. The basic feature of human personality is his freedom-unfettered and unrestrained.

Emphasis on Subjectivity. Kierkegard has emphasised the essentially subjective nature of human existence. It is based on man's insistence on the complete freedom and to choose and to become what he wills himself to become. Existentialism believes that alt human values are based on subjective experience.

Contingency of Human Life. Another significant concept of existentialism is the 'contingency' of human lire. Existentialism believes that existence of a person means his period from'birth to death. There was nothing before birth and would be nothing beyond death. This contingency is often characterised by experience of dread, horror, anguish, bewilderment, uncertainty and finally h u n t e d by death. Man is the only being in this world who knows that sometime he will die. He must learn to live with anguish, dread and anxiety.

Man is Basically Free. Existentialists prefer to view man as an indefinitely free responsible being. According to Sartre freedom is identical with existence. This infinite freedom puts up on him heavy sense of responsibility."

Self-knowledge. Existentialists believe that man should get an opportunity to know his self-realisation. Self-realisation makes the inner life of man the centre of concentration, free from anxiety.

Man is not Complete. For the existentialists, man is not - complete; he is in the process of'becoming'. Man has to meet challenge. He marches on the process of becoming a complete man to reach his completeness.

No Acceptance of Readymade Concepts. Existentialists believe that man cannot accept the readymade concepts of existence forced upon him. He is a free agent capable of'shaping his own We and choosing his own destiny.

No Faith in Absolute Values. Existentialists do not believe in absolute values They argue that as long as empirical spirit remains alive, it must remain open to revision and correction and hence it cannot adhere to fixed values. All values emerge from personal awareness, personal consciousness and personal experiences.

Existentialism

Educational Implications of Existentialism : Existentialism has very little to offer as a philosophy of education. In other words, "The philosophy of existentialism has not dispalyed any particular interest in education. Even Kneller feels that existentialists do not carry their doctrine into practical theory or policy for school behaviour."

Meaning of Education

In a broad sense, education is that which helps an individual to realise the best that he is capable of.

In doing so education must help the individual to realise the contingency of his existence, to face the categories of this facticity-dread, anguish, anxiety and fear-resolutely and courageously and finally prepare him to meet death with pleasure.

Existentialists speak of a new kind of education-education for death as compared to the idea of education for pleasure or complete living.

Existentialism and Aims of Education

Growth of Uniqueness in Man. Existentialists accept the psychological point of view that every individual is unique. Education must also cater to the needs of individual differences and help him tc blossom as an individual.

Man is Free by Nature. Education must make pupil aware of the infinite possibilities of his freedom and the responsibilities it must bear in mind. Education must help him have the capacity for self-direction.

Developing a Scale of Values. Education must develop in the pupil a scale of values consistent with his absolute freedpm, The pupil must develop a commitment to these values and act accordingly

"An uncompromising affirmation of authentic freedom an individual uniqueness is the message of existentialism to the phitosophy of education."

Another aim of education is the making of a human person as one who lives and makes decisions about .what he will do and be.

Existentialism and Methods of Teaching

Socratic Method. Existentialists favour the, Socratic approach to teaching as Socratic method is personal and intimate affair."

Here knowledge and wisdom are gained through mutual interaction of two living-beings.

Methods of teaching must be adjusted to individual differences and must give more individual attention.

Learning by Doing. Existentialists favour learning by doing as Sarte says, "The world and man reveal themselves by their understanding."

Emphasis on Origtnatity and Creativity. The teacher should facilitate development of originality and creativity by providing necesary material and equipment.

Methods of teaching must develop the creative atttities in children. 'Education for creativity" is of most Importance to the existentialists.

Group Method of Teaching mut be Avoided. Existentialists reject the group methods, because they supress the injdividual initiative and creativity.

No Intellectual Goals. In terms of fundamentals of existentialism, it is more important to develop the affectfve side of life-that is the emotional and aesthetic side of man than the rational or cognitive side of life.

Education must enable the pupils with a degree of internal perceptions and strength so that they are able to bear the pressure of the life of crisis.

Developing power of Self-observation. Development of introspective powers should also be the aim of education.

Existentialism and Curriculum

Existenitialists do not believe in prescribing a curriculum, pupil must choose his own curriculum according to his needs, abilities and station of life.

Curriculum should be related to the immediate social, economic, political and other group problems which the individual will have to face. Curriculum should include the subjects given ahead:-

Study of Humanities. Existentialists give more importance to humanistic studies than to the scientific subject as ft is through humanities that man comes to terms with human suffenng like anguish, anxiety and death.

Humanities help man to keep more closely to himself than science.

Curriculum should also include:

Social sciences, Moral and religious education.

Existentialism and Teacher

The role of the teacher in an existentialist scheme of education is very delicate. He must be the person who is himself authenticating his existence at every moment of his Rfe who has developed a consistent scale of values and is committed to it.

1. Teacher must not impose his own values upon his pupils. His supreme duty is to make his pupils understand the meaning and purpose of existence. He should be busy awakening awareness and freedom in his pupils.
2. Teacher must be sympathetic towards his students. Children must be treated as free individuals. Sympathy must be shown for their rebellious nature. For according to existentialists, a rebel is more moral than the conformist because he is authenticating his existence.
3. There are no problems with children. Teacher must enter into the emotional life of children. He must be sensitive to the emotional behaviour of children.

Existentialism and Discipline

Existentialists are opposed to any kind of prescription or any set rules for children. They are opposed to the practice of giving incentives, rewards or punishment to the pupils. They stand for absolute freedom in educational institutions. To be a man is to be free. Hence pupils must have complete freedom of choice and action in the school.

An Assessment of Existentialism

Existentialism has come into strong criticism from a number of quarters. The following points need a special mention:

1. The educational methods in existentialism appear to be impractical and inapplicable in an industrial society.
2. The idea of absolute freedom is not acceptable in the present social set up.

3. It requires a good deal of time and effort on the part of teacher to develop individual relationship with the students for having a closer understanding of their personalities.
4. It under-rates the attitude towards scientific inquiry.
5. Existentialism ignores the cognitive side of life and over stresses the affective side of life.
6. Terminology used in existentialism is not very dear. Concepts like 'Being', 'Meaning', 'Person', 'Existence' are ambiguous.

Thus we find that the philosophy of existentialism has its good and bad points looks their philosophies. But we cannot that it is a growing young philosophy.

Assignments

1. How has idealism influenced educational theory and practice? Discuss fully by giving suitable examples.
2. What are the salient features of idealism as a philosophy of education? Discuss.
3. "Idealism has more to contribute to the aims and objectives of education than to its methods." Discuss.
4. "Idealism shifts the emphasis from the the natural or scientific facts of life to the spiritual aspects of human experiences." Discuss by giving examples.
5. What do you understand by Naturalism in education? Discuss the impact of naturalism on educational theory and practice.
6. Discuss briefly the contribution of Naturalism to educational theory and practice.
7. What is Naturalism? Compare and contrast the aims and methods of Naturalism and Pragmatism.
8. Discuss the contribution of pragmatism to the educational thought. How far is it practicable in the Indian schools?
9. Critically evaluate pragmatic philosophy of education with reference to aims, methods and curriculum.
10. What are the underlying principles of pragmatism as a philosophy of education?

11. Pragmatism is midway between Idealism and Naturalism. Discuss.
12. What is existentialism? Discuss the fundamentals of existentialism as a philosophy of education.
13. "Existentialism is a growing young school of philosophy." Discuss and bring out the limitations of existentialism.
14. What are the educational implications of existentialism as a philosophy?
15. What is Existentialism? What are its educational implications?
16. What is the contribution of existentialism to contemporary educational thought and practice?
17. What are the basic ideas on which philosophy of existential rests? What are their implications for education?
18. What are the ingredients of the existentialistic philosophy of education. Elaborate its implications with regard to the major questions of education.

5

Role of Elders

To us, thoughts of great men reveal that we can also make our lives sublime. Great men become great through their unique thoughts in the social set up of life through which they come out leaving ever tasting impact on the foot prints of time. Their great thoughts and their great deeds make them great. Overnight they do not become great. They struggle in the teeth of opposition, bear hardships of life, sacrifice a lot and they are able to get name and fame. They give io the world something really good and useful. It is of unique importance as it suits the times and the social set up of life. It is in the larger interest of humanity. Surely the people, not only of that era but all times give due recognition to them, their ideology, their philosophy of life and their thoughts. They set the examples, give directions to the people and also set the path for others to be followed.

Educational thoughts of Mahatma Gandhi, Rabindra Nath Tagore and Swami Vivekanand have left behind glories on the foot prints of time which are keeping them ever alive. Their remarkable thoughts have everlasting impact on the whole humanity in the galaxy of great, these persons were great in their own unique ways. Mahatma Gandhi was really a Mahan Atma who worked for humanity, got India free from the shackles of Britishers. About Education, he said, "It ought to be for the children a kind of insurance against unemployment." His belief in 'learning by dong' and non-violence won him a great name. Rabindra Nath Tagore was a great lover of humanity and spiritual and his Vishwa Bharti present everything in its purest form. It is a combination of home and temple, unification of East and West, and above all, creation of international brotherhood on this pious land. Swami Vivekananda, the great social reformer, advocated self knowledge through concentration, character building and man making education. His discourses on philosophy and religion and his love for humanism have left everlasting effects in this universe.

Mahatma Gandhi (1869-1948

Mohan Dass Karam Chand Gandhi was a great leader, a practical philosopher and an eduationat thinker of great repute. He wanted to establish a free and casteless society with no exploitation and racial discrimination. For this purpose, he used education as an instrument. His philosophy of education was the outcome of his long experiences of political, social and economic life of the country.

Brief Life Sketch

Mahatma Gandhi was born on 2nd October, 1869 at Porbander in Gujarat. His father was a Dewan of Rajkot. After completing his studies upto Matric, he went to England for studying law. He passed his Law examination and was called to the bar in 1891. He did not do well here. In 1893, he went to South Africa as legal advisor. There he resisted for twenty years the inhuman treatment of the British Government against the Indians in a non-vilotent way.

In 1914, Gandhiji returned to India and continued his educational experiments for a short time at Shantiniketan and then at Sabarmati and Sewagram. It was here that Gandhiji not only conceived the idea of his new system of education but also fought his battle for freedom. He continued his efforts in liberating India in a number of ways. A few wonderful events of his times are Non-co-operation Movement after the Jallianwala Bagh Massacre, Quit India Movement, his historic fast of 1931 etc. He died on January 30, 1948 at the hands of a fanatic Nathu Ram Godse.

Gandhi's Philosophy of Life

Gandhi did not claim any original philosophy. His philosophy is however, based on the philosophy of Idealism. A brief description of some of his philosophical ideals is given below:

His belief in God. He believed in God unquestionably. God is the all pervasive Reality. Like an idealist Gandhiji believed, "God is that indefinable something which we all feel but which we do not know. To me God is Truth and Love. God is Ethics and Morality. God is fearlessness. God is the source of light and Ifie"

Sense of Human Unity. Gandhi advocated that as the source of all the rays of the sun is the absolute and one whole, in the same way though the persons are different, yet the same light prevades in all of them. He experienced and realised unity in diversity. '

Truth. To Gandhiji truth is the supreme principle. The realisation of truth is the only way to realise God. According to Gandhiji, God is Truth and Truth is God. Truth has a divine significance and is manifested in the voice of the conscience. Truth should be the basis of the whole life.

Non-Violence (Ahimsa). It is the second main tenet of his philosophy of life. Ahimsa is the only means to realise truth and God. To him Truth and Ahimsa are the two sides of the same coin. It is practically impossible to disintegrate and separate them.

Love. Love is the core of Gandhian philosophy. He advocated that the true religion of man was the religion of love. His love attained the form of universal love.

Brotherhood of Man. His motto was, "Thou shalt love thy neighbour as thyself." He wanted to establish a universal community of free persons without racial discrimination and artificial barriers of caste and creed. He had firm faith in the gospel of brotherhood of man.

Satyagraha. Satyagraha is the practical application of non-violence. It is a method of securing a right by personal suffering. It is to achieve change of heart by self-suffering by the adherence of truth and non-violence. It is the vindication of truth not by inflicting of suffering on the opponent but on one's self.

Service to Humanity. Service for humanity is the core of his philosophy. His greatest creed was service of God through service of humanity. For Gandhi, God lives in the temple of humanity. Man becomes great when he works for the welfare of his fellow men. He stated, "I shall work for an India in which the poorest shall feel that it is their country. In whose making they have an effective voice....an India in which all communities shall live in perfect harmony.

As a true philosopher, he could not help being an educator with the object of realising his ideal of a spiritual society; as a stepping stone of the realisation of God or Truth. He evolved an educational system as a dynamic side of his philosophy."

Gandhiji's Education Philosophy

Gandhiji evolved a philosophy of education as the dynamic side of his philosophy of life. He viewed education as a potent instrument of social reconstruction. On account of his new scheme of education known as 'Basic Education', Gandhiji is considered as the starting point of modern educational theory and practice of the East.

Meaning of Education

Gandhiji observes, "By education I mean an all-round drawing out of the best in child and man-body, mind and spirit. Literacy is neither the beginning nor the end of education. This is only a means through which man and woman can be educated." This is how Gandhiji summed up his idea of true education accordingly.

Education is development. "All round" implies harmonious development. 'Drawing out'of the best' recognises a great potentiality coiled up in the child which can be realised and developed to Its perfection through education.

It is development of human personality in terms of physical, intellectual and spiritual aspects. Education should take care of the whole child, the human personality.

It should be the function of education to bring about a harmonious development of all the aspects of human personality so that it can grow to Its highest stature and serve the society at its best.

Education is not Literacy. Gandhiji did not favour teaching and learning of as literacy in itself is no education. Literacy is just a means of education. He emphasized the development of head, heart, hand and health.

According to Gandhiji "true education is that which draws out and stimulates the spiritual, intellectual and physical faculties of the children."

Salient Features of Gandhiji Educational Philosophy

The salient features of Gandhian Educational philosophy are given below:

A new concept of education. Gandhiji interpreted education as the development of human personality. This can be matched with any modern concept of education. His scheme of education is life centred, it is education of life, through life and for life. It really provides opportunity for character building, development of all round personality and prepares for effective and successful living through life problems and real life situations.

It is Education for Citizenship. In the words of Dr. Zakir Hussain, "The new scheme which we are advocating will aim at giving the citizens of the future a keen desire of personal worth, dignity and efficiency and will strength in them the desire for self-improvement and social services i a co-operative communtiy."

Education for a new Social Order. Gandhiji wanted to make education an instrument of social change and social reconstruct on. By educating the masses, he wanted to establish a new society known as "Sarvodaya Samaj" - classless, casteless society. This society will be based on the principles of truth and non-violence in individual and collective life.

Practical Nature of Educaton. Gandhiji introudced craft centred or work oriented education which is the under current of any modern system of education. Though he had a desire to teach all the subjects through hand-work, he was never the less aware that everyone of these subjects could not be·so taught. He would not dogmatically interpret his scheme of education as education through crafts. "Craft is taught not for craft's sake but for opening up avenues of creative self-expression, practical work and learning by doing."

Gandhiji combined in himself the visionary and practical man. He was an idealist, naturalist as well as pragmatist. He was a man experimenting with truth.'

Psychologically Sound. His scheme of education is psychologically sound. It is based upon the fact that the whole educational structure be planned with the child as the centre. It implies different theories and laws of learning.

Sociologically Sound. Gandhian scheme of education inculcates the feeling, working co-operatively and fosters group life and building social qualities. It instill essential social virtues, builds character and provides better understanding of social life and its problems

It Solves the Problem of Unemployment. The scheme is economically sound as it leads to self-sufficiency which is the crying need of the day. It generates the feeling that work is worship. It is work-oriented education.

Sound Teaching Techniques. The methods of teaching especially the techniques of correlation are very sound. The methods and techniques of teaching advocated by him revolutionized Indian thinking.

In all we find that Gandhian philosophy of education combines in it all the philosophical trend's and tendencies, thus giving rise to the theory of education which would suit the needs of the day and satisfy the loftiest aspirations of the human soul.

Limitations

Gandhian philosophy of education which underlies the Basic scheme of education has been criticised on account of the following limitations:

The theory of Self-Supporting. It lays emphasis on child labour. Education of child in terms of his personality development would be neglected.

Waste of Material. Mahatma said that small children are not in a position to produce something worth-while. There is enormous waste of material.

As Trade Centre. Schools would be trade-centres.

Cruel Attitude. It is a cruel attitwie towards children.

Missing Ideal. Young children cannot be given the ideal of earning money during the period of elementary education.

Hindrance. It may arrest child's spontaneous development.

Old system. It is an out-dated and out-moded system of education.

Forced Correlation. Correlation becomes forced and and unnatural.

Aims of Education

Gandhiji divided educational aims into two categories such as:

1. Immediate Aims of Education and
2. Ultimate Aims of Education.

Immediate Aims

Vocational Aim. It is also Known as self-supporting aim of education. Gandhiji wanted that each child should be able to learn a productive craft to meet his future needs of life and become self-supporting. He advocated education for self-reliance and capacity to earn one's livelihood. In his own words, "Education ought to be for them (children) a kind of insurance against unemployment."

Cultural Aim. He advocated that vocational education and cultural advancement should go side by side. He considered the cultural aspect of education as more essential than its academic aspect. Culture is the main foundation and an essential part of education. In the words of Gandhiji, "I attach more importance to cultural factor of education than its literary factor. Culture Is primary and basic thing which the girls should receive from school."

Character Aim. According to Gandhiji, the end of all knowledge should be the building up of character. Character building implies cultivation of moral values such as courage, strength of mind, righteousness, self-restraint and service of humantiy.

Perfect Development Aim. Gandhiji once wrote, "The real education is that which fully develops the body, mind and soul of children." He further observed, "Man is neither mere intellect, nor the gross animals body, nor heart or soul alone. A proper and harmonious contribution of all the three is required for the making of the whole man and constitutes the true economics of education."

Dignity of Labour. Gandhiji wished that all individuals especially the learners should do some manual work. Studies are important at their own place. The students must learn the dignity of labour. They should not feel shy while doing some work with their hands.

Training for Leadership. Gandhiji believed that for successful democracy, good leaders are needed. Education should imbibe the education of good leaders. That way only the students will be able to shoulder the responsibilties in a satisfactory manner.

Individual and Social Aims. Gandhiji stressed that education should equip the learner for individual and social aims. Both these aims should be synthesised. That way only the individual becomes better and the society is enriched. Only good individual forms a better society.

Ultimate Aim of Education

Spiritual Development. Self-realisation and spiritual development find perfect support in Gandhian scheme. According to Gandhi, "Development of the moral character, development of the whole- all were directed towards the realization of the ultimate reality- the merger of the finite being into the infinite." It is realizing Godliness in his self.

His ideal of self-realization combines both the development- individual as well as the social. In the words of Mahatma Gandhi, "A nation cannot advance without the unit of which it is composed and conversely, an individual cannot advance without the nation of which he is a part."

Gandhiji and Curriculum

Gandhiji devised a scheme of eduation which is known as 'Basic Education' 'Nai Talim' or Wardha Scheme of Education'. Its curriculum is activity centred. He suggested the following subjects to be included in the curriculum:

Basic Craft. Gandhi prescribed productive craft as the medium of education. A number of crafts such as agriculture, spinning and weaving, wood work, metal work, gardening, leather work have been suggested.

Mother-tongue. Gandhiji stressed that all elementary education must be imparted through the medium of the mother-tongue. The proper teaching of mother-tongue is the foundation of all education.

Arithmetic. To be correlated with life situations, other subjects to be included in the curriculum are Social Studies, General Sciences, Art, Music, Drawing and Hindustani. He suggested Home-Science for girls.

Method of Teaching

Gandhiji advocated the following methods of teaching:

Education Through Craft. Education through productive craft is the basic of Gandhian scheme of education. It is around this craft that all other subjects in the school will be taught.

Mother Tongue to be the Medium of Instruction. According to Gandhiji, all education should take place through the medium of mother-tongue. It makes the process of education natural and meaningful.

Emphasis on Activity Mehtod. Gandhian education is not bookish in nature. Education is imparted through creative and productive activities.

Learning by Doing. Learning by doing is the watch word of Gandhian system of education. Thus the child participates in some activity and learns through experiences.

Technique of Correlation. Basic education envisages that the whole instruction should be imparted through the medium of some activity, experience or craft. This technique or procedure is known as the technique of correlation.

It is based on the principle of integration. Knowledge is an integrated one. To divide knowledge into compartments is educationally wrong. Correlation is an attempt to overcome isolated in mental life and removes artificial barriers of subjects.

Thus in the Gandhian scheme of teaching, academic contents are correlated with actual life experiences, environements and craft.

Lecture method, questioning and discussions are some more techniques which are employed in the Gandhian scheme of education as and when considered appropriate.

In short, stress should be laid on the principle of cooperative activity, planning, initiative and individual responsibility in learning.

Concept of Discipline

Gandhiji's approach to discipline is based on discipline of mind, thought and action. It is inner discipline or self-control. Discipline springs from within. Like naturalists Gandhi also advocated freedom for the child.

At the same time, he wants children to be prepared to accept the appropriate discipline and training.

His concept of discipline was in tune with social discipline. Education was recognised as a means for generating 'we feelings' among the individuals so as to make them useful and responsible citizens of the country.

Views about Teacher

Gandhiji wanted right type of teachers dedicated to their profession and ready to serve the masses. Teachers must be well-trained, proficient, men of knowledge, faith and enthusiasm. They must be patriots, men of character and nationalists.

Views about Women Education

Gandhiji was strongly in favour of women education. Women education can help in uplifting the society and the nation. Their best role can be in the education of the children. He said, "My greatest hope is in women. They want a helping hand to lift them out of the hell in which they have been kept."

Gandhi as Naturalist, Idealist and Pragmatist

On the basis of Gandhian approach to education, Gandhi has been described as a naturalist, Idealist and pragmatist.

Gandhi as Naturalist

Like Rousseau, Gandhi also believed that natural and rural environments were important educative agencies. He also agreed with Rousseau that the child is good by nature. Education must be child centred. He also advocates freedom for the child. That is why, he greatly emphasised the importance of educating the child in natural surroundings. He equally decried book learning.

Gandhiji as Pragmatist

Gandhiji's educational philosophy is pragmatic due to the following reasons:

1. He has an experimental approach towards life.
2. He advocates like a pragmatist that a child should learn from the real experiments of life and through life problems and situations.

3. The project method of the pragmatist and the basic scheme of Gandhi have many common points.

Gandhiji as an Idealist

In the words of Dr. M.S. Patel, "A study of his writings will lead to the conclusion that Gandhiji is an idealist to the core." Idealism is ingrained deeply in his nature as can be seen from his upbringing and early education.

Gandhiji attached great importance to the training of spirit. He says, "To develop the spirit is to build character and to enable one to work towards a knowledge of God and self-realization...... all training without culture of the spirit was no use and might be even harmuful," Like all other ideals, Gandhiji believes in the harmonious development of human personality.

Gandhiji very successfully synthesised different philosphies of education and emerged as a naturalist, idealist and a pragmatist. Dr. M.S. Patel rightly concludes, "Gandhiji's philosphy of education is naturalistic in Its setting, idealistic in its aims and pragmatic in its methods and programme of work."

Mahatma Gandhi and Basic Education

Historical Background

1. A Basic education was advocated by M.K. Gandhi in 1937.

   To quote Gandhi :

   "By education, I mean an all round drawing out the best in child and man—body, mind and spirit."

2. M.K. Gandhi published an article on basic education in "Harijan" in July, 1937.

3. Shortly after the publication of the article on basic education in "Harijan", in 1937, a conference was held with Dr. Zakir Hussain as Chairman for the preparation of tentative scheme syllabus for basic education. The recommendations of the Zakir Hussain Committee on basic education are listed here :

   (1) Provision of free and compulsory education for seven years to all children.

   (2) Mother-tongue as the medium of instruction.

(3) Education should involve mannual work, productive work or vocational work through art and craft methods of waching.

(4) Self-reliant/self-supporting aspect/concept must be kept in view.

4. The recommendations of Zakir Hussain Committee on basic education were examined by a Committee under the Chairmanship of shri B.G. Kher. This Committee was appointed by the Central Advisory Board of Education.

Central Advisory Board of Education appointed another committee under the Chairmanship of B.G. Kher to examine basic education in relation to higher education.

The report of the committee was published in 1944. The report was entitled as Post-War Development in India. The scheme of basic education according to this report is as follows :

— Provision of tree and compulsory education for children of age group 6-14, (eight years education)

Basic education should be in two stages.

— A senior stage (first five years)

— A Senior stage (three years)

Medium of instruction should be mother tongue.

Emphasis on manual work and productive work through craft methods of teaching.

The selection of crafts, and learner physical and social environment must be taken into consideration.

School should involve itself in the sale of the products of the school children.

There will be internal system of evaluation of the learners. There should no external examination.

Use of text books should be avoided as far as possible.

Emphasis should be given on cleanliness, health, citizenship, work, worship, play, recreation etc.

Teaching of different subjects for the harmonious and balanced development of the learners.

Salient Features

The term "basic" is used to convey meaning in context of the following references :

— Education should be based upon Indian culture.

— Education should be based upon nature and interest of the learners. The selection of activities for education should be linked with basic nature. The extension in academic activities should start from this criteria.

— Education should be given to every child up to the level catted as 'basic education level' irrespective of caste, creed or colour.

— Education for the primary period of one's education in one's life.

— Education is basic because it involves basic necessities of life-food, shelter and clothing. Educational aims, curriculum, methods, school environment role of teacher etc. are derived from these points.

— Education is linked with basic, urge for the learners at this age for creative work.

2. **Meeting the Needs of Indian Society.** To Quote Gandhi on basic education : "Spearheads of a silent social revolution, nurseries of truly free democracy. It will provide a healthy and moral basis between the city and the village and thus go a long way towards eradicating some of the worst evils of the present social insecurity and poisoned relationship between the classes."

The above quotation of Gandhi points out that basic education is derived on the basic needs of India people or society the needs of Indian society taken into consideration are as follows:

1. The three basic needs are food, shelter and clothing. Education is linked with these three basic needs with specific reference to Indian society.
2. Social development of the learners.
3. Teaching of democratic values through work, centred activities. For example sharing of responsibility like cleanliness, preparation and serving the food, participation

in the goverance of the situations/programmes, activities for well-being of the community. All there activities develop respect for work and the worker.

4. Development of "we-feeling."
5. Practical activities are designed to minimise the gap between social gap in the manual activities and intellectual activities. Sense of dignity of labour.
6. The education should develop faith in truth, ahimsa, equality, non-exploitation, non-violence.

Basic education uses Art and Craft Methods (Handicraft) of Teaching. The education, according to Gandhi, is drawing out the best in the child the body, mind and the soul. The method of teaching is through the scientic study of crafts. The contents of various subjects (History, Geography, Mathematics etc.) should be through craft methods of teaching.

Use natural, social and social environment is emphasized. The thinking skills, observation skills and physical skills are properly correlated.

Education is Self-relient and Self-supporting. Schools as Factories or Vocational Centres.

'Learning and earning simulanously :' is one of major central themes of basic education. The schools should perform the role of a producer as well as consumer of the products produced using arts and crafts methodologies of teaching. Self-sufficiency, vocational training, liberal education or general education, etc are all properly correlated.

Training for Citizenship. Following qualities are developed which are considered essential for a citizen in the Indian democracy.

— Development of sense of warmth, dignity and efficiency.

— Development of a desire for self-improvement.

— Development of a desire for doing something for the social development.

— Development of attitudes, appreciations for social problems values of a democratic society.

— Development of habits of mutual co-operation, mutual understanding, working collectively for production.

— Development of skills for democratic self-government in schools.

— Development of political leadership and sense of civil rights and duties.

— Development of appreciation for dignity of labour.

Curriculum

1. Spinning and weaving.
2. Gardening and agriculture.
3. Book craft.
4. Paper work.
5. Cardboard work.
6. Metal work.
7. Leather work.
8. Clay modelling.
9. Pottery.
10. Fisheries.
11. Home craft.
12. Mother tongue.
13. Social Studies.
14. Mathematics.
15. Arts unctuding drawing, music and aesthetics.
16. Hindi
17. Games.
18. Physical Education.
19. Time allocation for different content areas should be as shown in given following table.

TABLE

Time allocation for various subject (Basic Education)

Subject	*Grade*	*Time*
Craft	I—Ill	2 Hrs. a day
	IV—V	2 Hrs. a day
	VI—VIII	3 Hrs. a day
Mother Tongue	All Grades	40 Minutes a day
Social Studies & General Science	All Grades	1 Hour a day
Mathematics		20 Minutes a day
Art		40 Minutes a day
Physical Activities		20 Minutes a day

Limitations of Basic Education

Teacher Education. Teacher education programmes were not perfect. Teachers have no clarity of the concept of basic education.

Wrong Conception about Basic Education. Basic education was wrongly takes as educational programme for lower classes. This was not the case in the real sense. It was a full scheme for all sectors of the society for the purpose of individual development, and development of the Indian society at large.

Lack of Understanding about Craft Methodologies. The teachers, heads, and others linked with basic education were having no clear cut idea of crafts and their use as scientific and mechanical methods of teaching in realising goals of basic education. Secondary importance to contents of various subjects and literacy.

Secondary importance was given to literacy of the age of 6-14. Contents of various subjects were also not given due place in the curriculum.

Theoretically only Baric Education was activity oriented, but not in Real Situation. In real practical situation the basic education was not practical and vocational oriented. The implementation part is defective.

Poor Place to Art as Compared to Craft. Art was not given the due place in the curriculum.

Quality of Skill Developed in Learners was poor. The quality of skills (craftmanship and specific vocational skills were not very fine) of the learner was not upto the standard.

Parity problems for the students of Basic Education. Parity problems were faced by the students of basic education for further education. Students who studied in other educational systems were preferred for higher educational levels. This affected basic education programmes adversely.

Rabindra Nath Tagore (1861-1941)

Rabindra Nath Tagore has been one of the topmost edcuationists of India. His name will ever shine like a star in the galaxy of educationists who contributed handsomely to the cause of education. His thoughts on education are worth studying.

A Brief Life Sketch

Rabindra Nath Tagore, well known Indian saint, was born on 9th May, 1861 in Calcutta. He was the youngest son of Maharishi Devinder Nath Tagore who was a great Brahmo SamaJ leader. In childhood, Rabindra Nath was educated at home by a private tutor. The father taught him Upani' shads, Astronomy and Sanskrit. Then he received education in St. Xavier's School Calcutta. He hated the routine type of teaching conducted in the school. Rather he called the schools took learning factories'. The father sent him to England at the age of 16 to study law. There also he did not do well. He developed taste for English literature and soon started writing poems. He was only 20 when his first collection of poems was published.

His experiences of life helped him to form his own philosophy of education. In 1901, he established a school 'Shanti Niketan' which later became a world famous University - Vishwa Bharti University'. His classic work 'Gitanjaii' won him the Nobel Prize for literature in 1913. The University of Calcutta conferred upon him the honorary degree of D. Litt. In 1913. This great literary figure who was also a philosopher and prophet of humanity breathed his last on August 7, 1941. He was really a great lover of humanity.

His Philosophy of Life

Tagore was a naturalist comparable to Rousseau because he

had full faith in God and nature. He was of the view that every individual should be given freedom to grow and develop as per his own wishes. About his educational scheme he clearly said, "Education divorced from Nature has brought untold harm to young children."

He was a realist and an idealist too. But in no way and to any extent was he a materialist. His realism is reflected when he says, "Our education should be in full touch with our complete life, economic, intellectual, aesthetic, social and spiritual and our educational institutions should be very near of our society." And his idealism can be seen when he says, "Let us find God, let us live for the ultimate truth which emancipates us from the bondage of the dust and gives us the wealth, not of thing but of inner urge, not of power but of love." About his idealistic philosophy Dr. Radhakrishanan said, "The soul of ancient India is mirrored in Tagore's writings. It embodies all the ancient ideals of religion, philosophy and art."

He believed in the oneness of humanity. He was deadly against untouchability. He was a true patriot. He had all regards for all the religions of the world. Besides, he believed in the harmony between the East and the West and above all, he was a true Vedantist.

Educational Philosophy

Tagore's philosophy of life gives reflections of his educational philosophy. He was fully dissatisfied with the system of education. He called the schools as factories of role learning. They were all impractical type and stood far away from the prevailing social set-up of life.

Basic Principles of his Philosophy of Education

Principle of Harmonious Relations. Tagore believed in harmonious relationship of man with man, with surroundings-nature etc and in international relations. A man through the process of education should be able to come out as a harmonious individual in tune with his social set-up of life. Tagore rightly says. "The highest education is that which does not merely give us information but makes our life in harmony with all existence."

Principle of Freedom. He was of the view that the children should be given freedom so that they are able to grow and develop as per their own wishes. Let there be freedom of mind, freedom of heart and freedom of will. They help to have spontaneous self-expression. In such an environment of freedom, nature will teach and teach very well making the individual a successful person in his social set up of life. To him education is that which liberates an individual.

Principle of Creative Self-expression. Tagore was not in favour of mere intellectual development. He stressed that education should promote creative self-expression. He suggested that creative self-expression could be promoted through subjects like craft, music, drawing and dramatics. The environment of freedom given to the learner and then creating situations for him will automatically make the learner do something original. He said, "Hand work and arts are the spontaneous overflow of our deeper nature and spiritual significance."

Principle of Communication with Nature. Tagore recommended that education should be provided the company of nature. That will strengthen the ties between children and nature. Both man and nature are the creations of one Jnd the same God. This will naturaly strengthen spiritual relationships between the two. Thus his naturalism was different from the one advocated by Rousseau. The difference being that Tagore's naturalism was based on humanism. 'Love and harmony among all the things that exist in nature' was the basis of his eduational philosophy.

Thus we can conclude about Tagore's views on education as:

1. "Reformatory and extensive process which seeks to unfold all that is good and noble to individual.
2. "The highest education is that which does not merely give us information but makes our life in harmony with all existence."
3. "Education is a permanent part of the venture of life. It is not like a painful hospital treatment of curing students'of the malady of their ignorance, but it is a function of the health, the natural expression of their minds."

Aim of Education

Aims of Education, as per the philosophy of Tagore are as under:

Physical Development. Tagore strongly believed that good health is a must for the (earner, *A* sound mind is present in a hale and hearty learner. Education must help the learner to grow and develop fully. It should help the learner have good physique. Physical development leads to all round development of the personality.

Moral and Spiritual Development. Moral and spiritual development is another important aim of education. Some types of moral training must be given to the learners. Education should enable a person to work with self-determination. The more a person is morally and spiritually sound, the more dedicated and devoted he becomes. Mental satisfaction and peace of soul should be embedded in the education.

Intellectual Development. The great Indian saint was against bookish knowledge. He did not like the schooling process as it was traditional one laying stress on cramming by the learners. He advocated that type of education which would help the individual to have free thinking. It should develop the imagination power of the students.

Harmonious Development. Education should help the individual to have all round development. He did not like that education which developed one aspect of personality fully and ignored the others. His firm faith was that education should help the individual have harmonious development of personality. That way only, complete manhood could be attained.

Purposeful and Meaningful Education. Education which is imparted to the students should be meaningful in the context of their existence. It should always have a useful purpose to serve. It should help them grow well and come out successful in the situation they are ever placed in. It should help them solve problems of day to day life.

International Understanding. Tagore believed in universal brotherhood and oneness of all human beings on this earth. International understanding, he said, could help in forging untiy among all. Therefore, he advocated that education should help in more and more international understanding. Tagore said, "Mankind must realise a unity, wider in range, deeper in sentiment, stronger in power than ever before." The main aims of Vishwabharti are to "Establish intimate relationship between the East and West to promote inter-cultural and inter-social understanding and to strive for the unification of mankind."

Harmony between individual and Social Aims. Tagore advocated that education should bring in harmony between the individual and social aims. An individual in isolation cannot come out as a fully grown and developed individual. Education should help the individual in making him realise that he is an integral part of the society. He is to exist in the society, grow and develop in society. Through this interaction, he should improve himself and the society. Tagore was humanist and he strongly advocated that education should bring harmony between the individual and social aims. Only that way self-realisation should be achieved.

Tagore's Views about Curriculum

Tagore was not in favour of existing curriculum as it was not good for the complete development of an individual. He said that the curriculum should be broad based. It should cater to the needs of the individual and the society. It should help in the complete development of the individual on one side and on the other hand, it should develop the spirit of nationalism and internationalism. He said that the curriculum "should consist of subjects of study, activities and actual living. The following are the details of the curriculum:

Subject of Study

Language and Literature. Mother tongue and other Indian languages, English and other foreign languages (ii) Mathematics (iii) Natural Sciences like Physics, Chemistry, Botany, Zoology, General Science and Health Education (iv) Social sciences like History, Civics, Geography, Economics and Sociology (v) Agriculture and Technical subjects (vi) Arts, Music, Dance, etc. (vi) Philosophy, Religion and Psychology.

Activities and Occupations. (i) Dancing (ii) Dramatics (iii) Music (iv) Games and Sports (v) Drawing and Painting (vi) Agriculture and Gardening (vii) Excursions (viii) Regional Study (ix) Laboratory Work (x) Social Service and (xi) Self-Government.

Actual Living and Community Service. The curriculum revolves round actual living and Community Service. Life at

Shantiniketan is a living example of this everybody there is an active member of the community and he/ she has to render social service. Manual labour and participation in community activities is a must for everyone there. Department of Rural Reconstruction is a centre of attraction for all this. *Tagore* very clearly said, "It must not only derive its contents but also its substance and inspiration from the social life at large." Thus in brief we can say that Tagore recommended comprehensive type of curriculum which helps in the complete development of man.

Methods of Teaching

Tagore was dissatisfied with the methods of teaching which were used in the institutions. He called those traditional methods as lifeless and unsuitable ones. His preaching was that the method/ methods should be in accordance with the needs of the individuals. Let individualised methods be used for teaching. That helps in proper growth and development of each individual. The following methods of teaching were recommended:

Teaching while Walking. Tagore said, "Teaching while walking is the best method." So he laid emphasis on tours and excursions. The students are able to see things and they have first hand information about things. They are able to understand well and can also retain it in their minds for a longer time.

Debate and Discussion Method. Tagore suggested that the learners should be encouraged to take active part in debates and discussions. Let there be no pouring knowledge into the mind of the student. Every topic in the classroom should be taught through discussions. Through discussions, many doubts are cleared. The learner is able to develop the power of clear-cut thinking. He also learns how to solve problems of day to day life.

Activity Method. Activity method activates the learner and makes him physically more sound. The different faculties of body and mind are better trained by this method. That is why Tagore proposed activities like jumping, climbing the trees, plucking fruit, clapping, dramatising etc.

Heuristic Method. This method is quite popular at Shantiniketan. Science and Mathematics are better taught by this method. In this method, the learner is in the position of a discoverer. The students are put in a situation and they ask questions from the teacher. The teacher clarifies points and answers their questions with the maturity of his thoughts. Later the teacher puts questions to the students in order to test their comprehension.

Concept of Discipline. Tagore did not like the theory of strict and harsh discipline. He was not at all in favour of any type of suppressions. He wanted free environment, freedom of mind and freedom in learning. The teacher should have a good deal of sympathy and love for the child. That will really teach the child and that will place the child on the right track. It will make the child self-disciplined. So self-disciplined learners are the heart-felt desire of this great educationist.

Views about Teacher. The teacher plays a very significant role in the education of the child. He is a Guru and he is expected to understand fully his disciples the learners. Only a good learner can be a good teacher. A real teacher is able to inspire and is ever ready to guide his students. Tagore rightly says, "He who has lost the child in himself is aboslutely unfit for the great work of educating the children." He further says, "A teacher can never truly teach unless he is still learning himself. A lamp can never light another lamp unless it continues to burn its own flame."

Shantiniketan or Vishwa Bharati

Tagore's Vishwa Bharati at Shantiniketan is a living symbol of his philosophy of life and education. In this educational institution, he gave practical shape to his ideas. In 1901, Tagore set up a school at Shantiniketan which was two miles from Bolpur in Bengal. Gradually over the years, it developed into Vishwa Bharati - an international Unviersity. It is an abode of peace where teachers and students live together in a spirit of perfect comradeship. The motto of this institution is "Where the whole world forms its one single nest."

Shantiniketan has open spaces, atmosphere of freedom surrounded by natural enviornment. It is open to all irrespective of country, race, religion and politics. It is a self-governing institution. Size of the classes is small and so individual atttention is paid to every learner. They believe in simple living and high thinking. All around there prevades spiritual and religious atmosphere.

Aims of this Institution

(i) To bring the different cultures of the East into close contact with one another.

(ii) To provide new approach to Western Science and Culture.

(iii) To establish relationship between the East and the West by the study of their philosophy, cultures, art etc.

(iv) To provide education for the whole man.

(v) To provide opportunities for the freedom of mind, heart and will.

(vi) To help them have balanced development of different aspects such as physical, moral, spiritual, intellectual etc.

Shanti Niketan and Rabindra Nath Tagore

Establishment in 1901. Shantiniketan was started by Tagore in 1901 Shantiniketan is situated near Bolpur, a place about one hundred miles from Calcutta (West Bengal).

It was started as an experimental school in the Shantiniketan Ashrama (abode of peace) of Tagore's father. Maharishi Devendra Nath, the father of Rabindernath Tagore established Shantiniketan Ashram in 1863. Father of Tagore permitted Tagore to start Shantiniketan in 1901 which was elevated to Visvabharati (the international University) in 1921.

Principles of Education. To quote Tagore about ideals of Shantiniketan :

"To give spiritual culture to our boys was my principal object in starting my school at Bolpur. Fortunately in India, we have the model before us in the tradition of our ancient forest schools, where teachers whose aim was to realize their lives in God, had their home. Having in my mind this ideal of a school which should be a home and a temple in one, where teaching should be part of a worshipful life. I selected this spot, away from all distractions of town ; hallowed by the memory of a pious life whose days were passed there in communion with God."

"This first help that our boys get here on this path is from the cultivation of love of nature and sympathy with all living creatures. Music is very great assistance to them, songs being not of the ordinary hymn type dry and didactic, but as full of lyric joy as another could make them..."

Love for natural environment, use of mother tongue for imparting knowledge, freedom, sympathy with all living creatures, songs full of joy, spiritual development of the learner, creative self-expression, active communion with nature, man and god etc. are the principles/ideals on which Shantiniketan is based.

Open Air Classes. The principles of education of Tagore do not favour holding classes within the four walls of the class-room. Principles of freedom of young children, communion with nature and God, love for surrounding etc. can be implemented only if the classes are held in open air. Nothing is so free as air, and nothing is so inspiring as sky.

Co-education and Residential Nature. It is co-educational and residential type educational institution. The environment in general can be assessed on the basis of following features.

— Co-education.

— Residential nature.

— Students live together.

— Students have community meals.

— Student work together.

— There is no consideration of caste and creed.

— Food is cooked together and served.

— Life is simple and cheap.

— Students work with their hands generally (cleaning of rooms), washing of clothes and utensils.

Management of student. Management of the routine functions is done by students of quote

"However great a scholar one may be, if he has not educated his body, he has to live a life of dependance on others, in many mays, he is an incomplete man.

Working Hours. Working of the school starts at 5 am. Students get 90 minutes for their routine personal work. They get breakfast.

Regular classes are held up to 10 a.m.

Lunch break

Regular classes after lunch.

Curriculum. Ordinary school subjects

Crafts (Sewing book-binding ; weaving ; carpentary

Projects

Music

Dance

Fine arts (Drawing and art)

Experimental science

(Provision of laboratories is there for conducting practicals.)

Medium of Instruction. Mother tongue was the medium of instruction.

Hobbies and Occupations. Students were free to pass their leisure time in hobbies and select occupations of their choice.

Wide Reading. Reading was not restricted to text books but wide reading was encouraged.

Freedom, Internal Discipline and No Punishment. Freedom and sense of responsibility are the underlying basis of discipline i.e. Internal discipline was encouraged. No punishment was given. Confession of the mistake is sufficient and repetition of mistake is avoided.

Home like Environment.

* "Home" is the term that was used by Tagore for his school generally.
* Teacher and students used to live and play together.
* Married teacher used to invite students at home and treated them as their own children.
* No strict classroom discipline.
* No fixed rules
* To quote Tagore :

  "I never said to them," Don't do this or don't do that. I never prevented them from climbing trees or going where

> they liked, I wanted to make children happy in an atmosphere of freedom."

Number of Students in the Class. Number of students in a class was small. Teacher thus had the opportunity to understand the children in their class.

The rapport between teachers and student was there.

Problem of Children. Problem children were handled by Tagore himsetf. Love and environment of freedom solved all problems.

Organisation of Extra-Currrcular Activities

* Organisation of dramas, Musical Concerts, Art exhibitions, Dance
* Songs on seasonal festivals

Manual Labour. Dignity of manual labour was taught by Tagore. Students were engaged in routine manual activities e.g. cleaning and dusting of rooms, cheaning of utensils, fetching water from well.

Development of Awareness about Economic Aspects. Tagore advised people for cultivation of land, importance of science, training to students in industrial aspects. The above efforts on the part of Tagore were to develop economic awareness among people and students.

Efforts for Development of Village Life. Tagore took necessary steps for the development of life style in villages. In this context, he emphasized on village industry, (weaving, carpentary, pottery, leather-work, paper-making, etc.) agriculture developmental activities, and steps for happy and humane life in villages.

Visvabharati (1921). The Shantiniketan was elevated to the centre of higher learning popularly known as 'Visavabharati' on 22 December 1921. It was the first international University in India.

Central Aims of Visvabharati. The central goal of Visavabharati was to establish a relationship between East and West and to promote inter-cultural and inter-social amity and understanding and fulfill the highest mission of the present age- the unification of mankind.

Constituent Units and Vishvabharati. A few names of the constituent units of Vishvabharati are liked below:

1. Sisu Bhavan (Nursery School)
2. Path Bhavan (School Section Matriculation Examination)
3. Siksha Bhavan (Higher Education)
4. Vidya-Bhavan (College of Undergraduate and Postgraduate Studies and Research)
5. Vinaya Bhavan (College of Teaching)
6. Kala Bhavan (College of Fine Arts and Dance)
7. Sangit Bhavan (College of Music and Dance)
8. Shniketan (Department of Rural Reconstruction)
9. Sikra Satra (Rural High School)
10. Silpa Sadan (College of industrial Training)
11. Cheena Bhavan (School of Languages e.g. Chinese, Tibetan etc.)

Social change through Education. Tagore emphasized on the change in society through education. He wanted to modernize India by making use of education as an instrument by combining the best of East and West. The manners, customs and art of India can be combined with western arts and sciences.

Swami Vivekananda

Narendra Nath Dutt was born at Calcutta in 1863. He belonged to a kshatriya family of Calcutta. His father Shri Vishnu Nath Dutt was an advocate in Calcutta High Court. His mother Bhuvaneshwari Devi was a pious woman. He was fortunate to learn many things from his parents. From the beginning, he had great love for languages, philosophy and music. During his schooling days, his Headmaster W.W. Haesty gave his impression about Narendra Nath in the words : "I have travelled far and wide, but I have not met such an intelligent and scholarly student even in German Universities." The Headmaster once talked about the famous spiritual leader Shri Ramakrishna. Thereafter his love for spiritualism made him a follower of Swami Ramakrishna Parma Hansa. It made him a monk and then he was known as Swami Vivekananada.

Swami Vivekanand a spread the gospel of Ramakrishna Paramhansa and explained the philosophy of Vedanta to the Americans and the European public. He had full sympathy for the poor and (down- trodden. He wanted to teach Vedanata to every one without any distinction of caste, colour, creed and sex. He respected every religion. To him, no religion was inferior to the other. To him, Hindu civilization was good, spiritual and beautiful.

Swamiji was a great advocate of a national system of edcuation. He was in favour of education of the masses. He wanted to educate the women and thereby he wanted to improve their plight in the society. He was not in favour of role learning from the books. He wanted to promote spiritualism, perfection, divinity) self-reliance, universal brotherhood and faith through education.

The great religious saint and social reformer died in 1902 when he was just 39 years. He is no more but he will be remembered for ever on this earth. His missions and his preachings will continue inspiring the coming generations

From the complete Works of Swami Vivekananda (7 volumes) Advaita Ashram, Aimora, 1947- here below are reproduced a few times:

"We want that education by which character is formed, strength of mind is increased, the intellect is expanded and by which one stands on one's own feet."

"All great accomplishments are hard. Nothing worth-while comes easy. But don't lower the ideal because it is difficult to attain. Hold the banner of freedom aloft.......Strength ! Strength ! Strength ! Say that to yourself day and night. You are the strong ! The Pure ! The free ! No weakness in you, no sin, no misery !"

"God comes to those who work hard. God helps them that help themselves. An opposite idea of God weakens our nerves, softens our muscles, makes us dependent. Everything independent is happy; everything dependent is miserable. Man has infinite powers within himself and he can realise it, he can realise himself as the one infinite self......."

Swami Vivekananda's Karma Yoga

In the Essay "The Secret of Work" the following extracts highlight his views:

He gives here the true message of work. We should take work as worship. We should do the work selflessly and without any attachment. He says miseries of the world cannot be cured by physical help. They will continue untill there is change in man's character. Ignorance causes evil and misery in life. It can be removed only if mankind gets spiritual light true education and pure character.

Vivekanand ephasises the value to good thoughts, good impressions and good actions. These are the basis of good character. Good tendencies should replace bad tendencies. Good thoughts should rise again and again until the evil ones disappear. One should practice mercy in life and regard work as worship.

The desire for liberation is the high stage. It means freedom from the bondage of good as well as evil. Swami Vivekanand gives a beautiful example, A person, has a thorn in his finger. He uses another thorn to take it out. After taking it out, he throws away both the thorns. Similarly good tendencies are used to remove bad one. When bad tendencies disappear, there is no need of any tendencies good or bad. That is liberation-non attachment. One goes on doing good actions.

Swami Vivekanda reminds us that the world is not our permanent home. It is only one of the many stages through which we are passing. We should, therefore, not attach ourselves to any worldly thing. We should think that we have come here only to do some work. We should do it constantly and feel free from the bondage of the wortd.

Real existence, real knowledge and real love are closely linked with one another. These are the three aspects of God which we call Existence-Knowledge-Bliss.

Swami Vivekananda says that we should take the position of a giver in life. We should give everything as a free offering to the world. We should not wish for any reward or return. This will lead us to unattachment and real bliss.

There are two things which guide the conduct of man:

Night and Mercy. The exercise of might is always an act of selfishness. But mercy is heavenly. We have to be merciful in order to be good.

The lotus lives in water, but its leaves are not touched by it. Similarly, a selfless man may live in the very heart of a crowded and sinful city, yet he will not be touched by sin.

Educational Philosophy of Swami Vivekanada

Concept of Education. Swami Vivekananda defined Education as "the manifestation of divine perfection already in man." He believed in to learning or self-learning. The role of the teacher is only that of a facilitator or a guide only. The teacher only motivates or encourages the student and thus he helps him in finding out the hidden treasure of knowledge already present within him.

Book learning, rote learning or filling the mind of the students with lot of information is not education at all. According to him, "Education is not the amount of information one gets but it is life building, man making, character forming and assimilation of ideas." He was against the theoretical type of education."

Aims of Education. According to Swami Vivekananda: "The end of all training should be man-making." Education should help in bringing about all round development of an individual. Further he rightly says, "Blessed are the men and women whose minds are centred on the acquisition of knowledge, who possess sweet and amicable tempers, who cultivate truthfulness and other similar virtues, who are engaged in altruistic work as prescribed by the Vedas."

The different aims of education as advocated by Swami Vivekananda are as under:-

1. Education for strong Moral Character. Education should develop strong moral character of an individual. It should not be just filling in the mind of the learner with all type of so called knowledge only. The whole beauty of life is linked with it. Purity of thought, work and deeds come out of it.

2. Education for Self-realization. Education should help an individual so that he/she is to realise about himself.

   Freedom, liberty and salvation are the hall marks of life.

   Education should help in the attainment of the said ideals of life.

Education for Self-reliance. Self reliance is the most important thing for everybody on this earth. Self-dependent finds ecstasy everywhere and in every way within his ownself. Education should make a person self-reliant.

Education for Promoting Universal Brotherhood. Universal brotherhood is very essential for peace, prosperity and progress of an individual. Education should help in promoting universal brotherhood. According to Vivekananda "Through education, we should gradually reach the idea of universal brotherhood by flinging down the walls of separation and inequality........"

Education for Physical Development. A physically strong person is the need of the society. Brahamcharya helps in becoming physically strong and stout. Education should help in the physical development of an individual.

Education for Religious Development. 'Humanity and your service to if should be the religion of all individuals on this earth. That education is worthwhile develops such feelings in the learners.

Curriculum

What type of curriculum is all right for the students becomes dear from the following words given by Swami Vivekananda:

"My idea of education is personal contact with the teacher-Gurugraha-Vasa. Without the pe: sonal life of teacher, there could be no education."

Teacher's home and what ever prevails there should be the curriculum for the learners. Swami Vivekananda did not prescribe any specific type of curriculum. But there is no doubt that Swami Ji wanted all round development of the individuals.

That included moral, physical and spiritual development of the individuals.

He was in favour of the study of Vedanta, Religion, Philosophy and Theology. Secondly he wanted science, engineering and technical subjects. Thirdly, he wished that games, sports and physical exercises should be the integral part of the curriculum. And above all, he wanted that ti e curriculum should suit the needs and requirements of the masses.

Method of Teaching

Swami Vivekananda believed in the inner knowledge of tht student. According to him, pouring in from outside in the individual was no real education. Everything is within the individual and that comes out to the individual by the method of concentration. He was in favour of practical methods and not, the theoretical methods. His belief was that the learner should have all reverence for the teacher. His faith or Shardha in the teacher will make him learn anything and every thing well.

The following methods were recommended by Swami Ji:

Self-Study. The teacher should be the facilitator. He should help in creating the environment which will help the student do self study. The real example of the teacher with this regard will also do.

Meditation and concentration are very near to each other. Every individual should be trained for concentration. Of course, concentration depends upon Brahamcharya. Practice of concentrating will help the student learn more and more.

Discussion Method. Swami Ji advocated discussion method of teaching. The teacher should involve all the students in the discussion. There should be free and frank discussion between the teacher and the learners on different students in the discussion. There should be free and frank discussion between the teacher and the learners on different topics of study. That will serve the purpose of education fully.

Thus we find that Swami Ji was in favour of practical methods that helps the individuals to learn tilings interestingly and also with their self efforts. There the teacher provided just guidance to them.

Role of the Teacher

The teacher is a friend, philosopher and guide to the students. He with his own example imbibes in the students all good things. The personal life of the teacher is of much more importance than the knowledge he possesses. Only a selfless person can be good teacher. The teacher should be pure at heart and he should be a dedicated one.

Swami Ji wanted that the teacher preaches religion and he should impart secular education to the people.

Swami Vivekanada believed in self-teaching. He said that every one was his own teacher. In this regard Swami Ji's words are worth quoting. He says, "As is the plant, so is the child. The growth and development of plant and child takes place according to their nature. The role of external teacher lies in helping the pupils so that they may learn to apply their own intellect to the proper use of their hands, legs, ears and eyes."

Women Education

Swami Vivekananda laid special emphasis on the education of the women. On women education alone depends the prosperity of a nation. He very, c l eariy said, "There is no hope of rise for that family or country where there is no education of women, where they live in sadness. For this reason, they have to be raised first."

He preached for equal rights between men and women. He rightly said, "The best thermometer to the progress of a nation is its treatment of its women."

Swamiji was disappointed to see the poor plight of the women in India. It was rather shocking for him to know that man had not given them rights equal to them. He pleaded the case of women for their uplift. He asked the women to draw inspirations and learn lessons from the great women of ancient India i.e. Rani of Jhansi, Meera, Savitri etc. His strong belief was the uplift of women alone could raise the status of the family. Therefore, he suggested that more and more schools be set up for educating the women.

Man Making Education and Vivekanand

Humanism, The central Goal of Man Making Education. Upliftment of humanity (humanism) is the central goal of man making education of Vivekanand. This is because of his thinking that God realisation is only through service of humanity.

The above central goal can be achieved through a variety of effects/steps. A few examples are :

- Provision of free and compulsory education for the people.
- Formulation of National System of Education that may emphasize Indian culture.
- Formulation of policy for women education.

- Steps to check the problems of casteism and untouchability. Establishment of centres that may promote man making concept of education of Vivekanand. e.g. (1) The Rama Krishna Mission was established in 1899.

Activities of the Mission

— Relief work of any nature e.g. flood, famine, diseases.

— Opening of educational institutions (schools, colleges).

— Opening of hospitals.

— Programmes for the development of central goal i.e. man making education.

Vedanta Society. Vivekanand established the Vedanta Society in San Francisco for the purpose of spread of vedanta philosophy.

Aim of Education

Man making education means education that contributes to the development of inner man. Development of inner man helps us to come up from the state of poverty and helplessness.

Aims of man making education are as follows :

- **Development of Character**. Education should contribute to character building i.e. development of will power, that may lead us to courage, stamina and fearlessness.
- **Balanced Human Relationship**. Education should help us in acquiring skills that may help us to develop balanced human relationship.
- Self-confidence
- Self-reliance
- Adaptability to the challenges of changing society.
- **Spirituality.** Fellow feeling, sympathy and sharing and solution of common problems.
- Feeling of brotherhood and unity of mankind (Power of God exists in all).
- Service to humanity is service to God.
- **Work is worship:** work for hungry, ignorant and suffering masses.
- **Acquisition and spirit of renunciation:** leare materialistic outlook and develop love for knowledge and sacrifice.

- **Self sufficiency.** Practical training alongwith traditional religious and cultural training.

Curriculum. The curriculum should be need based and modern. A few aspects are mentioned here

1. Culture with specific reference to India.

— History
— Poetry
— Grammer
— Languages
— Lives of great men
— Vedantic Studies
— The Mahabharata
— Ramayana
— Ancient India
— Indian Languages
— English
— Commerce
— Psychology
— Cookery, Child-rearing, craft, economics & psychology for women only

2. Modern Science

3. Technology, and Engineering.

4. Synthesis of scientific pursuits of Vedas and Western pursuits.

Vocational Studies for Self-sufficiency

— Skills related to different vocations alongwith general studies.

— Vocational training should enable children to earn their livelihood/should make the children self-reliant.

Organisation, Administration and Management Training. Training in general aspects regarding organisation, administration and management should be included in the syllabus with the aim to expose learner to suctt training that may develop relevant skills for organisation and management of commerce, trade and industries in India. This will help in the upliftment of society.

Teaching Principles. Principles/Bases of the Methods of Teaching for Man Making Education are as follows :

1. Principle of Chastity and Celibacy are very significant for intellectual and spiritual growth of the learners.
2. Principle of faith in self. Self concept is very significant factor for learning.

3. Principle of reverance for the guru and great teachers. This is necessary from the viewpoint of the development of love in an individual for knowledge.
4. Principle of Meditation and Concentration. This helps an individual to check factors of distraction and acquisition of knowledge.

   Principle of humanity ; devotion to learning.

   Principle of attitudes of persistence in solving problems.

   Principle of self-sacrifice, kindness and gentleness towards others.

   Principle of development of relationship with guru (teachers) on the Guru-Shishya traditions of ancient India.

Guru-Shishya Method: Methods of teaching based upon Indian traditional Guru-Shishya traditions, the lecture method and book studies are inadequate ; personal examples and ideas of the teacher help more in the development of the learner.

Meditation Method: Concentration and Meditation-are prerequisite for studies.

Discussion Method :

— Open discussion on the contents of study.

— Questioning and inquiry spirit.

Travel Method. Exposure provide learning experiences. Teachers and students can learn more through travelling experiences within India and abroad.

The Teacher

Coming to the Level of the Learner. The teacher should come to the level of the learner. Teacher should think that he/she is to listen through the ears of the learner ; he/ she is to look through the eyes of the learner ; he/she is to think and understanding through the intellectual development of the learners. The above thinking of the teacher helps him/her to communicate and connect effectively with the learner and bring desirable changes in the learners.

Concept of Guru Grahayasa. Guru and the student should live in the same house called as Guru Grahayasa. Teacher should behave fatherly and set example/model useful for the intellectual, social moral and spiritual development of the learner.

Man making education and concept and Guru Grahayasa is gaining momentum in the advanced countries.

Love and Devotion to Humanity. Teacher's love is not limited to the learners alone but he/she prepares the learners for spreading the love for humanity. The teacher is for the development of the humanity.

- Self-Sacrifice
- No love for Materialism.
- Attitude of deep learning.
- Renunciation as aim of life.

Assignments

1. Describe the following about Mahatma Gandhi.
   (a) Philosophy of life.
   (b) Educational Philosophy.
2. Discuss the following in context of Mahatma Gandhi.
   (a) Aim of Education
   (b) Curriculum
   (c) Methods of Teaching
   (d) Disciplines
   (e) Teacher.
3. Discuss in detail basic education as advocated by M.K. Gandhi.
4. Discuss in detail educational philosophy of Rabindra Nath Tagore.
5. Describe Shanti Niketan taking into consideration all aspects advocated by Rabindra Nath Tagore.
6. Describe educational philosophy of Swami Vivekanand.
7. Discuss man making education in context of Swami Vivekanand.

6

Different Theories

Different Western thinkers like John Dewey, Froebel and Montessori have contributed significantly in the development of principles of education. These principles have provide us the direction to determine various aspects of educational theory and practice. e.g. aims of education, curriculum, methods of teaching, concept of school environment, concept of discipline, role of the learners, role of the teacher etc. The present chapter deals briefly the philosophies and educational philosophies of John Dewey, Froebel and Montessori. Special emphasis have been given on to John Dewey's learning by doing Frpabel's playway method and Montessori's didactic appartus.

John Dewey (1859-1952)

Great persons make great contributions and on that account they are remembered for all times. Some are born great, some become great through their workings and greatness is thrusted upon some. John Dewey was born in a poor family but he became great on the basis his works and great deeds. He stands today in the front rank of educationists of the world. He is by far the most original thinker in the field of educational philosophy. To him philosophy is not a passive contemplation but something which solves the problems of life. It is all due to him that today we find freedom, happiness and friendliness in American schools. Dewey is a philosopher of present time which is dominated by science, technology, industrialism and democracy. His approach to problems of life is original and he has offered sound solutions to great problems.

Brief Life Sketch

John Dewey was born in Vermont in England in 1859. His father was an ordinary shop-keeper. He was brought up in rural environment. He always participated in the discussions held at his father's shop. He disliked traditional methods of schooling. He had always something new and different to say at the time of discussions. In 1879, he graduated from Vermont University. He got his Ph.D. degree in philosophy at Johns Hopkins University. This enabled him to join the University at Michigan as a lecturer in philosophy. In 1894, he was appointed Head of the Department of Philosophy in the University of Chicago. Herein 1896, he founded his 'Experimental School" known as Laboratory School which won him world fame. His ideas had a considerable influence over the American system of education. From 1904 to 1930 he worked as a Professor of Philosophy at Columbia University. During this time he visited Japan, China, Turkey, Russia and many other countries. He also established himself as a prolific writer. He contributed articles of different types for educational journals and magazines. After his retirement, he remained as Professor Emeritus till his death in 1952.

John Dewey has a number of books to his credit, which have won him world wide fame. Some of his books are:

(a) A School and Society, (b) The School and the Child, (c) School of Tomorrow, (d) Democracy and Education. (e) The Child and the Curriculum, (f) Reconstruction in Philosophy. (g) Education Today (h) My Pedagogic Creed (i) Experience and Nature, (j) The Quest for Certainty, (k) Human Nature and Conduct etc. (I) An introduction to Social Psychology.

Philosophy

John Dewey was a pragmatist and an experimentalist. He was a practical thinker who did not consider philosophy as passive contemplation. According to him, philosophy could always solve the problems of life. The outstanding features of his philosophy are:

No Eternal Values. According to John Dewey, there are no eternal values. All values are relative and created by man in society. They are always changing. What is true today may cease to be true tommorow.

Truth is that which Works. John Dewey believed in workable type of truth only. It must fulfill the purpose.

Experience is the Core of his Philosophy. Experience is the only basis of reality and true knowledge. That is why his philosophy is all practical.

Thought and Action are Complementary. No doubt, action is always superior to thought, but at the same time thought and action are complementary.

Everything is Provisional. There is nothing in the world which is ever-lasting. Everything is provisional.

Faith in Democracy. Dewey's philosophy reflects the impact of democratic ideals. It is practicable only in a democratic set up. He had firm faith in democracy. He always advocated co-operative living. Dewey says, "The aim of living is the ever enduring process of perfecting and refining."

Relationship between Individual and Society. Dewey believed in the organic relationship between the individual and the society. Man or the self cannot grow in solitude. An individual must live with the rest of mankind. An individual is a citizen growing and thinking in a vast complex of relations. Society is indispensable for his development. In this context Dewey writes, "To learn to be human is to develop through the give and take of communication an effective sense of being an individually distinctive member of community."

Dewey's Instrumentalism. Dewey was an instrumentalist. Ideas are tools and instruments with him and they help in solving the problems of life.

Dewey's Experimentalism. He was also an experimentalist. He was of views that every idea should be tested by experiment before it is finally accepted.

Utilitarian view of Dewy. As a pargmatist, Oewey believes that experiences should be measured by the degree to which they function in meeting the actual needs of the individual and the society. Whatever is useful is good and whatever is good is useful.

Science and Scientific Method. His philosphy bears the impact of industrial revolution and machine. He, therefore, emphasised science and scientific method as they govern human affairs of all kinds.

In all Dewey's philosophy is based on the evolutionary concepts of Darwin and pragmatism of William Jones. He considered philosophy as the theory of education in its most general phases.

Dewey's Educational Philosophy

Dewey's educational philosophy fortifies his general philosophy and pragmatic approach to education. He defined education as the continuous reconstructton of experiences.

Meaning of Education

According to Dewey, "Eduction of all those capacity in the individual which will enable him to control his environment and fulfii his or responsibilities." He further contends that all education proceeds by participation of the individual in social consciousness of the race.

Two Sides of Education

Psychological. Dewey says, "Education must begin with a psychological insight into child's capacities, interest and habits." The psychological side is the starting point of all education. In the beginning, it is important to understand the psychology of the child in his interest, attitude, aptitude etc.

Sociological. Sociologist education is the process of socialisation of an individual. The basis of eduation is the interest of the child and those of the society. According to Dewey, "True education comes through the stimulation of the child's powers by the demands of social situations in which he finds himself."

Dewey and Aims of Education

Dewey did not believe in the fixed aims of education. The aim of education is to have more education. Aims of education should grow out of the life situations of an individual. He, however, emphasized individual and social aims of education.

Education helps in harmonious development of the individual. Dewey says, "I believe that education is a process of living and not a preparation for future living."

The aim of education, according to John Dewey is, "to produce socially efficient individuals. Social efficiency means cultivation of power to join freely in shared or common activities." Education should train the individuals in the art of living together.

According to John Dewey, the aims of education are as under:

Education as Growth. Education is the process of growth. It helps an individual to grow and develop. "Growth unlimited and illimitable" is the true object of education. This growth is not limited to physical growth. In the words of Dewey, "The process of education is a continuous process of adjustment, having as its aim at every stage an added capacity of growth."

Education as Life. According to Dewey, education is life and life is education. Life is a by-product of activities and education is born out of these activities. Education, in fact, is preparation of life through life experiences. School provides life experience to the child. By life, he meant social life and not individual life or personal life.

Education as social Efficiency. According to Dewey, "What nutrition and reproduction are to physiological life, education is to social." Man being a social animal develops through education, reasoning and social skills and becomes socially efficient.

Education is Continuous Reconstruction and Reorganisation of Experiences. According to Dewey, education is a process of living through continuous reconstruction of experiences. Education is by experience, for experience and of experience. Experiences are reorganised in the light of changing circumstances and problems of life. John Dewey rightly says, "We should so regulate the learning and experiencing activities of the young, that a newer and better society will arise in the end."

Concept of Curriculum

Like aims, curriculum should not be fixed or rigid. Curriculum should be developed on the basis of the following principles:

Principle of Flexibility. Curriculum should not be fixed once for all. It must be flexible and grow out of pupil's interests, impulses and experiences. It must reflect the social life of the child and his activities in society.

Principle of Utility. Curriculum must include those subjects, activities and experiences which have some utility and serve some useful pruposes. They must help in solving human problems and stand in good stead ultimately.

Principle of Child's Activities. Curriculum must be organised around the child's activities and not subjects. It should be related to child's contemporary experiences.

Principle of Integration. Dewey advocated that the subjects, activities and experiences should be integrated into one whole. Water tight compartmentalisation should be avoided. The mind of the child is a complete unity.

Methods of Teaching

Dewey has given his approach to class-room teaching in his works entitled, "How We Think" and "Interest and Efforts in Education". Here he contends that the best method of teaching is that which is based on learning by doing, and direct experiences. He remarks that all learning must come as a by-product of actions and never something learned directly for its own sake.

Methods of teaching should be based on the principles of natural interest, effort and motivation. Dewey advocated the following methods of teaching:

Project Method. Dewey recommended projects to be used as teaching technique. This lays emphasis on pupil's purpose, needs, interest, self-activity and participation in the entire process of teaching. A project is a purposeful activity proceeding in a social environment.

Problem-solving Method. Dewey also suggested that problematic situations should be provided to children in the class-room as- well as outside the class-room.

Experimental Method. His experimental method is in tune with Heuristic method. All learning should come as the by-product of experimentation.

Direct Experience and Activity Method. Dewey emphasized learning by doing and learning through participation. Direct experience is the basis of all the techniques of teaching.

In short Dewey advocated self-education, self-learning, play-way technique, children's interest and motivation. His significant contribution lies in his approach to class-room instruction based on effective learning, originality and initiative.

Concept of Discipline

Dewey criticized the traditional approach to discipline. He believed in self-discipline and social discipline. In other words, he believed in discipline which emanates from the cooperation in the social life.

Discipline is not the end. According to Dewey, the main purpose of school discipline is the cultivation in the pupils of social attitudes, habits and ideals of conduct through the joint activities of the school which have been organised as community.

Free Discipline. Dewey advocated free discipline. Such a discipline results out of free, purposeful and creative activities.

Teachers must not be Discipline Conscious. Teachers have to provide right kind of environment so that the child may find a scope to develop as a responsible member of the society. The teacher should not impose himself on the pupils. It should not be discipline for the sake of discipline.

Views About School

A teacher occupies an important place in the educative process. Dewey assigns a very responsible job to a teacher. A teacher is a friend, a guide and a helper. He has to observe, plan and encourage pupil's activities, environment and experiences.

A teacher must be professionally trained and an efficient person who has to lay the foundations of a successful social life. Besides the teacher should have sympathy for the child. In this regard, John -Dewey rightly says, "Since the teacher has presumably a great background of experience, there is some presumption of the right of the teacher to make suggestion as to what to do, as there is on the part of head carpenter to suggest to apprentices something of what they are to do."

Views about School

Dewey's concept of school was unique in all respects. School is a place where the child learns through his experiences. It is a place to live, learn and participate.

Dewey started his experimental school known as laboratory school at Chicago in 1896. It was like workshop. It was an ideal school representing his philosophy of education.

The following are the main features of an ideal school as conceived by John Dewey:

Extens on of Home. Dewey's ideal school is an extension of home. It means a school has to provide the same atmosphere of love and affection which prevails in the family.

A Miniature Society. An ideal school as conceived by Diwey is a community in itself. It cultivates in pupil's social consciousness and social loyalty. It is a small society, a society in miniature form.

School as a Specialised Institution. Education is a social process and school is a social institution. It provides specially controlled environment where children get knowledge for the processes of society and get acquainted with those ideals, faiths, attitudes, skills ctc.

School is a place to live, work and learn simultaneously. It is an idealised society.

Contributions of John Dewey

Dewey's contributions to modern educational theory and practice are remarkable. He brought about a revolution in the field of education. Many of his ideas have had a great impact on modern education. The following points need special mention:

1. Dewey has given a progressive outlook to education. Education is now regarded as life itself. 'Living' and 'doing' itself is education. It is preparation for life through life experiences.
2. Dewey has sufficiently stressed the social nature of education by pointing out that social efficiency is the aim in education. In other words, he emphasised 'socialisation' of an individual.
3. Dewey deserves the credit for emphasising that education should be child-centred. Study of the individual differences which forms the basis of the present education is his legacy.

4. We owe to Dewey the idea of 'core curriculum' and stressing the need for having an integrated curriculum. His concept of 'Activity Curriculum' is also very significant.
5. Dewey deserves the credit of inventing the Project Method of education.
6. Dewey rightly emphasised that morality and religion are no more theoretical subjects. These should be taught through practical experiences.
7. Dewey has brought in democracy in education. 'He held that school is small community in which children practice the art of living together. Education as such is to equip an individual in the art of successful and effective living.
8. It was Dewey who first started an experimental school in Chicago University. Today we find experimental school in every advanced country.

Learning by doing

According to John Dewey, "Learning by doing" is the principle on which method of teaching should be based. Besides the principle 'Learning by doing" following principles should also be considered as the based for teaching method.

1. Principle of activity.
2. Principle of purposefulness of activity.
3. Activity should be connected with life.

According to this principle, education should be imparted throught activities and practical experiences. Pragmatism believes in action and actual anticipation of the child in life situations. This principle stresses the fact that a child should be put into real situations and problems and should be enabled to study the situations intelligently and to solve them absolutely. The child gains insight and capacities to face and solve the problems of life.

Method Based upon Learning by Doing : Project Method

Kilpatrick, one of the followers of John Dewey defined project as a purposeful activity proceeding in a social environment. Stevenson defined project as a problematic act-carried to its completion in its natural setting. According to Ballard, "project is a bit of real life that is imparted into school."

Following are the steps of the Project Method :

1. Providing a situation.
2. Selection of the project and its delimitation.
3. Planning.
4. Execution.
5. Evaluation.
6. Reporting.

Criticism

John Dewey has been criticised on account of the following:

1. Absence of spiritual values. There is absence of spiritual values in the philosophy of John Dewey.
2. No clear aims of education. Dewey did not specify clear-cut aims of education. He emphasised "The only aim of education is to have more education."
3. There was too much empahsis on utility, practice and practicalism.
4. There was too much reliance on experimental method.
5. Project method is not suitable under all situations. It is vey expensive.
6. It puts heavy responsibility on the teacher.

Freidrich Froebel (1782-1862)

About Feroebel

1. **Early Period of Froebel**

* Friedrich Froebel was born in Germany in 1782.
* Mother of Froebel died during his infancy stage and his father neglected him.
* Uncle of Froebel adopted him at the age of eleven. Uncle of Froebel was on some important position in the Church.

2. **Education of Froebel**

* He got training as a forester at the age of 15.

* He spent two years in the forest alone and possibly developed deep love for nature and developed the habit of contemplation and observation.
* He studied for two years at the University of Jena.

3. Teaching Experience

* He joined as a teacher at Frankfort on main. He also tried other professions also. He was a successful teacher served Pestalozzi's school at Verdu for about three years.

4. Education in Berlin & Establishment of a school.

* He got further education in Berlin.
* He established a school in 1816 at Griesheim.
* School was shifted to Keilhau.
* He followed the method of education which was based upon Pestalozzi's principle of encouraging the learner to learn through self activity.
* School at Keilhau was successful.

5. Publication of Books. The Education of Man (1826).

Froebel published the book entitled "Education of Man' in 1826.

To quote Froebel from this book,

"The true method of education consists in considering the mind of the child as a living whole in which all the parts work together to produce harmonious unity."

6. Establishment of kindergarten using Play way Method of teaching. Froebel opened his first kindergarten at Blackenburg in 1827.

7. Extension Lectures and Training of teachers in line with Kindergarten. Froebel spoke on the philosophy of playway method and Kindergarten system at many places in Germany. He also imparted to teacher in the method & kindergarten system principles.

8. Governmental Dissatisfaction on the Socialistic views of Froebel. Government was not happy with the spread of socialistic views as a part of his Kindergarten system and playway method of teaching. He was checked to open schools based upon his principles.

9. Death. Froebel died in 1862. Froebel's grave is marked by a slab with a cube, cylinder and sphere on it.

10. Suitable saying for Forebel. "Come, let us live for our children." The playway method was advocated by Friedrich Froebel from Germany the founder of Kindergarten system of education for pre-school education of children of age group three to seven.

Philosophy of Education

The basic principles of Froebel's philosophy are briefly listed here with specific reference to playway method of teaching:

Principle of Spontaneous Development of the child.

1. Earliest years of a child are very important for the development of the child.
2. There is a similarity between a child and a plant. The child grows spontaneously just as the plant grows naturally.
3. The leaves and branches in a plant come up as determined by the material present in the seed. The growth of the child is also controlled by the child's tendencies and impulses present within him.
4. The child should be helped to develop by giving expression to the impulses which are hidden within him.
5. There is a need to identify the native interests and tendencies of children.
6. Self-activity is the chief quality of mind of the children.
7. Self-activity of the child expresses retief through play.
8. Development of the child is based upon play (manifestation of self-activity of the child)
9. Play is the most beautiful and most spiritual activity of man at this stage.
10. Play exhibits freedom and creative activity.

11. Play provides expression to many tendencies & instincts of the child.
12. Play helps the child to convert his internal into external.
13. Teaching during age group 3-7 should be in the environment of a play.
14. Child should be taught everything through play.
15. Freedom, play and joy fosters self expression.
16. Training in self expression is possible through songs, movement and construction.

Principle of Manual work & Handwork. Manual work and hand work helps the child in the development in the following ways:

1. Manual work and handwork develop muscles.
2. Creativity of the child develops.
3. Ideas and energies of the child are expressed.
4. Character building through work progresses.
5. There is a spiritual significance of the manual work.

Principle of Nature Study. Nature helps the child in the development of following characteristics:

1. Moral values are developed.
2. Religions spiritual development takes place.
3. Sense of appreciation for God for his creation in the mind of the child.

Principle of Sense Training

1. Senses receive the information from the surrounding and experiences with concrete items help the child to learn about them.
2. The maxim concrete to abstract being followed at this stage. Thinking (abstract) develops through concrete experiences (work n concrete objects).

Principle of Unity or Inter connectedness.

* There is an eternal unity i.e. God. All things have there origin in god, the eternal unity.

* Diversity of things in the world are interconnected.
* Man and nature are simply different forms of God. " There is diversity in Unity (God) and unity in diversity."
* Unity (God) can be viewed from three angles:
* Unity in substance (Man and nature are two different forms of God).
* Unity in origin (God is the source of origin of everything).
* Unity of purpose (All things strive to achieve divine perfection i.e. God).

Principle of Individuality through Process of Socialization.

* Personality of the child should be developed following the process of socialization.
* The child develops in social institutions i.e.,home, school religious places, the state. It is not possible to develop the individuality without these social institutions.

Aims of Education

1. Realisation of Unity i.e. God.
2. Realisation of Unity in Diversity and Diversity in Unity (God).
3. Channelisation of energies/impulses through self expression.
4. Development of the individuality of the child.
    * Physical development
    * Intellectual development
    * Emotional development
    * Social development
    * Spiritual development.
5. Environmental awareness
6. Nature study
7. Development to value system (justice, truth, loyaltiy, co-operation)
8. Development of good habits of action, feeling and thinking.

9. Development of well defined concepts (form, number, addition, etc.) physical skills & social skills.

Curriculum

Assumption about curriculum

1. Playway activities linked with songs, rhymes and gifts.
2. Miscellaneous Playway activities e.g. Manual work, Natural sciences, Languages, Art, Religion, Vocations and Mathematics.
3. Scholastic education in case of children of age group (3-7) leads to laziness.
4. Manual work is necessary condition for the realisation of child's personality.
5. Nature study creates sense of wonder and admiration in the minds of children for the work of God.
6. Natural science including Mathematics develops understanding of laws of nature.
7. Religion and spirituality is the core of all eduation.
8. Language acts as a link among various forms in nature.
9. Arts provides oportunities for self-expression.

The Play Way Method

Playway Doctrine of Froebel. Forebel based the education of the child (3-7 years) on play by identifying play and work as one i.e teaching through playway. This play way doctrine has wide educational implications. Today, playway doctrine or pedagogi or methodology is being used in a number of academic activities at various levels in schools.

To quote Forebel

"Play is the characteristic activity of the childhood. It is the highest phase of child development of human -development, for it is self-active representation or the inner representation of the inner form, inner necessity and impulse. Play is the purest, most spiritual activity of man at this stage and at the same time, typical of human life as a whole-of the inner, natural life in man and all things. It gives, joy, freedom, contentment, inner and outer rest and peace with the world. It hold the source of all that is good."

Playway Activities. Play activities in the Kindergarten system of education can be categorised by the teacher on the basis of instructional objectives. Teacher is responsible fo designing, directing and guiding functions in context of play activities.

To quote Froebel about teacher here:

"Without rational, conscious guidance, childish activity degenerates into aimless play instead of preparing for those tasks of life for which it is destined. Without law abiding guidance there is no free development."

Song/Rhyme Playway Activities. Song/Rhyme playway activities (mother songs and nursery songs) are arranged by the teacher in accordance with the development of the child.

Each song has three parts:

1 The motto (for the guidance of the mother or the teacher).

2. The verse with the accompanying music (for the child)

3. The picture (for illustrating the verse for the child).

Songs/Rhymes-based Playway Activities

1. Songs (50 in numbers) connected with nursery games e.g. Hide and Seek.
2. Rhymes (Nursery Rhymes) e.g. Humpty Dumpty, Jack and Jill, Cyndrella.

Instructional Objective

1. Provision of exercise to child's senses, limbs and muscles.
2. Development of familiarity with objects around the child.
3. Physical intellectual and moral development.

Playway Activities connected with Gifts

The gifts are used for designing a variety of playway activities linked with specific instructional objectives. The gift based playway activities & their corresponding instructional objectives are summarised below for the purpose of clarification & the playway method of Froebel:

TABLE
Gift based playway activities and objectives

Gift No.	*Components of the gift.*	*Activity Required or occupation*	*Instructional Objective**
Gift 1	Six coloured wooden balls. Three balls are coloured with primary colours i.e red, yellow and blue. Three balls are coloured with secondary colours i.e. orange, green and purple.	Children are required to roll these coloured wooden balls in playway attitude or mood.	Children are expected to attain the concept of colour (primary and secondary colours) -Concept of form -Concept of motion -Concept of direction -Concept of muscular sensitivity
Gift 2	* One sphere • One cube • One cylinder These forms are made of hard wooden form during his - play with these given forms.	Children are required to focus or notice on the stability of each 2. Children are expected to diff- -erentiate between stability and mo- -billty.	1. Children are expected to attain or learn the concepts of stability and mobility.
Gift 3	One large cube divided into eight smaller equal cubes (it is also called the first building box containing cubes) e.g. benches, steps, door,	Children will be occupied in playway mood on the activity of bull- ding useful artistic forms purpose of buidling specific forms.	Students are expected to attain the concepts of addition and subtraction through playway handling of cubes for the
Gift 4	Large cube divided into eight oblong prisms. Each prism has	Children are invovled or occupied in the playway	Children are expected to attain concept of pattern and design of

Gift No.	*Components of the gift.*	*Activity Required or occupation*	*Instructional Objective**
	length twice its breadth and the breadth twice its thickness.	construction activities i.e. building of a variety of patterns and buildings using light oblong prisms.	various forms.
Gift -5 (Gift-3 & 4 are also given alongwith gift-5)	It consists of a large cube that is divided into 27 small cubes. Three of the 27 small cubes are divided further diagonally into halves. Three of the 27 cubes are further subdivided into halves. Three of the 27 are further subdivided into quarters.	Children are directed to engage themselves in an atmosphere of playway activities concerning development of a variety of forms and patterns using components of gift 3, gift 4, and gift 5.	Children are expected to attain the concepts of form and number through playway activities of gift 3 gift 4 and gift -5
Gift 6 (similar to gift 4)	Large cube divided into eighteen wholes and nine small oblong blocks. materials.	Children are directed to developers designs using the given gift	Children are expected to attain the concept of number.
Gift 7	A set of triangular and square tablets of very fine wood in two geometrical forms different colours.	Children are directed to prepare geometrical forms and mosaic work.	Children are expected to attain the concept of mosaic.

List of the gifts that are provided to children for occupying or engaging them in a well-directed playway activities with predetermined instructional objectives:

1. Gifts 1-7 (see Table) (explained in the given
2. Stick-laying
3. Perforating
4. Paper cutting
5. Threading of beads
6. Mat-making
7. Embroidery
8. Basket-making
9. Wire work
10. Drawing and Painting
11. Modelling

Steps to be followed by the teacher for Playway Method:

Planning. Teacher must plan his/her lesson. Following points must be taken care of for getting useful results of he palyway activities:

- Selection of song/gift or both
- Writing objectives of the playway activity.
- Organisation of the material e.g. the illustration of the verse (in case of song), the component parts of the specific gift (in case of gift for playway activity).
- Rehearsal of the demonstration of song/gift playway activity for the students.
- Rehearsal of the song linked with gift activity.
- Specification of the role during playway activities (active role is required)

Execution of Planning.

1. Teacher directs the students and gives necessary instruction.
2. Teacher demonstrates the playway activity.

3. Teachers ask children to work on the given task.
4. Teachers actively observes encourage children.

Evaluation. Teacher evaluates children in the development of required skills. The feedback helps the teacher to replan and rethink about his/her role while in action with the children engaged in playway activities.

Duties of the Teacher

Following are the duties of a teacher in using playway method of teaching with specific reference to Kindergarten philosophy of Froebel:

1. Teacher should help the children to realise their impulses by using the encouraging behaviour or behaviours of practise and appreciation during the playway activities.
2. Teacher must demonstrate the playway activity before engaging students in the specified activity.
3. Song/rhyme linked with gift activity should also be demonstrated by the teacher.
4. Teacher should develop moral qualities self-control, etc.
5. Teacher should plan his/her lessons taking care of all aspects e.g. instructional objectives, materials required, demonstration, specific duties in an activity, evaluation etc.

Merits of Play way Method

Playway activities (Playway songs, playway activities with gifts, playway construction activities etc.) in the Forebel's Kindergarten system of education for the pre-school phase (age group 3-7 years), contribute to the development of the child in the following ways:

Cultivation of Good Habits. Good habits of action, feeling and thinking can be cultivated through playway song activities, gift related playway activities and construction/occupation playway activities.

Songs to related playway activities for awareness about the objects around the child. The playway activities specifically on songs enable the child to use his senses, limbs and muscles and this enables him to develop familiarity with objects in his surroundings.

Satisfaction of physical, intellectual and moral needs of the child. Playway songs/activities related to songs contribute to the child's satisfaction and as a result of the physical, intellectual and moral development takes place in the desired direction.

Development of Understanding about Basic Concepts. Understanding about the following basic concepts is possible in the children at this stage (3-7 years).

* Concept of colour
* Concept of form
* Concept of motion
* Concept of muscular senstivity
* Concepts of stability and mobility.
* Concepts of addition and subtraction.
* Concepts of pattern and design.
* Concept of form
* Concepts of numbers
* Concept of mosaic form
* Concept of geometrical pattern

Development of Psychomotor Skills. Psychomotor skills (physical skills) can be developed that are linked with playway handling materials e.g.

* Paper cutting
* Drawing and painting
* Clay modelling.
* Mat-making
* Wire work.

Development of values. Value system can be developed e.g.

* Justice
* Truth

* Loyality
* Co-operation
* Perseverance
* Consideration for others.
* Freedom
* Value of wisdom.
* Faith in God.
* Unity & diversity of God.
* Social values.

Development of the Individuality of the child. The individuality of the child can be developed in the desired direction through well directed physical, intellectual, emotional, social and spiritual development.

Nature Study. Activities provide opportunities to the child to understand the nature e.g. gardening activities, drawings on natural aspects.

Development of Senses. Senses are developed through activities: These are the important gates of learning. It these are sharp, then data collection from the surrounding is received well. Thus learning is enhanced.

Limitations of Playway Method

Some criticism on the following lines is there:

1. It is difficult to understand the Froebel's views.
2. Development is caused by external environmental conditions. Internal factors like impulses do not play role in the development of the child.
3. The material suggested for playway activities is outdated. It should be revised.
4. Gift activities are not relevant today. These must be purposeful and relevant.
5. Sense training can be given effectively by many other means.

6. Project method & other methods are useful for linking various subjects.

Contributions of Froebel to Educational Theory and Practice.

1. Use of Playway methods/approach in educational areas.
2. Emphasis on nursery education.
3. Self-activity in education.
4. Respect for the child's individuality.
5. Learning through arts and craft.
6. Emphasis on sociological basis of education.
7. Emphasis on philosophical basis of education.
8. Emphasis on sense training.
9. Emphasis on nature study.
10. Emphasis on religious and spiritual education.
11. Development of Kindergarten (The child's garden), system of educaton.
12. Channelisation of child's impulses & instincts through self-expression playway activities.
13. Emphasis on the maxim "concrete to abstract." This is for teachers as a maxim of teaching for making teaching effective and goal oriented.
14. Emphasis on the teaching of various occupations or vocations in the form of playway activities.

Maria Montessori (1870-1952)

Life Sketch

1. Dr. Maria Montessori was born in July, 1870.
2. She got MD degree from University of Rome.
3. She served at Psychiatric Clinic of University of Rome.
4. She was the incharge of feeble minded children at Psychiatric Clinic.
5. She observed that feeble minded condition of the children was due to dullness of senses. Sense training was given by help.

6. The observation on sense training encouraged her to extend her studies on normal children of age group 3-7.
7. She opened a school called as Children's House in 1907.
8. She used her method of sense training.
9. She emphasized on physiological data e.g. record regarding weight, height and other bodily measurements.

Principles of Montessori Method

Principles on which Montessori method is based are as follows:

Unfolding of the Child's Individuality.

To quote Montessori "If any eduational act is to be efficatious, it will be only that which tends to help towards the complete unfolding of the child's individuality."

The individuality of the child is to be unfolded through eduation. Teacher should guide & perform the desired roles. This principle is in line with that of Froebel.

Principle of Spontaneous Development of the Child Through Full Freedom. Freedom is essential for growth & development of the child. Freedom is the fundamental right of the child. Freedom helps the child to learn independence. Freedom to the child is also pleaded on two bases:

First basis of freedom for children. School must study the child and for this purpose, freedom should be given to the child.

Second Reason. Discipline comes through freedom only. Discipline is self-control that comes through self-activity in the atmosphere of freedom.

The Principle of Self-Education or Auto Education. Self-education is the best method by which the child learns in his own way and at his own rate.

1. The whole course of the child education is to be impersonal so that no conflict might arise between the desire of the teacher and that of the child.
2. Auto education means that no teacher is necessary.
3. Didactic apparatus was suggested by Montessori for controlling the error /mistake done by the child.

Principle of Muscular or Motor Training. The muscular activities like writing, walking and running help the child to depend upon himself and to do things himself from a very early age.

Principle of Training of Senses. Senses are the gateways of knowledge. Dr. Montessori, on the basis of her studies observed that senses of children of age group 3-7 years are comparatively active and consequently a great deal of learning takes place during this period. Intellectual development is dependent upon one's ability to make fine sensory discrimination. The attentton of the child is dependent upon the sensory stimulus but not on reasoning or thinking. Emphasis should be given on stimuli that sensitises for weight, colour, sound, touch and temperature.

Principle of Metamorphosis (Physical Metamorphosis and Psychological Metamorphosis). The term "Metamorphosis" was used by Dr. Montessori with reference to the following context:

To quote Montessori:

"The child is in a state of continuous and intense transformation of both body and mind, whereas the adult has reached the norm of the species".

The above change from child's state of body and mind to the state of body and mind of an adult is called as metamorphosis.

The change in context of body is called as physical metamorphosis while that of mind is called as psychological metamorphosis.

The principle of metamorphosis both physical and psychological emphasizes on the whole way of dealing with the child. Physical exercises should be given due attention during the years 3-7. The psychological metamorphosis attaches importance to child's love for activity and spontaneous repetition.

Didactic Apparatus and the Montessori Method of Teaching

The Montessori method of teaching uses didactic apparatus for development of motor sensory and language skills. The use of didactic apparatus in the Montessori method is described in three parts.

1. Didactic Apparatus and Development of Motor/Muscular skills (Motor Education)

Aims of Motor Education. Motor/muscular education involves the acquisition of motor skills with specific reference to following movements-

- Walking movements.
- Sitting movements.
- Movements in relation to holding of objects.
- Movements in relation to the care of the child's own body.
- Movements for managing the house.
- Movement for gardening activities.
- Rhythmic movements.

2. Use of Didactic apparatus.

Didactic apparatus is used for developing motor skills. For example following motor skills are developed with the help of didactic apparatus:

TABLE
Didactic Apparatus and Motor skills

Didactic Apparatus	*Role of the teacher*	*Motor skill Development*
A number of frames are there as a part of didactic apparatus. The pieces of clothes and leather are attached with these frames.	The teacher helps the child to perform the movements required for species pieces of clothes and leather & child enjoys in the movements.	Children are engaged in different movements e.g. button closing/opening & other movements.

The child is taught various other skills besides motor skills on a variety of pieces of clothes and leather. For example:

1. Learning of movements used in washing and laying of a table.

Children undertake a variety of movements (motor exercises) based upon following tasks/activities:

* Gardening
* Washing of faces

* Polishing of shoes
* Brushing the carpets.
* Polishing of metalware.
* Laying the table & placing crockery on it without any damage to crockery.
* Modelling activities.
* Making of tiles and bricks with simple moulds.
* Walking in line (provide rhythmic movement).

Didactic Apparatus for Sensory Training

1.**Didactic Apparatus :** Details, Didactic apparatus or sensory training consists of the following items:

* Solid insets (three sets)
* Three sets of solid in graduated sizes.

- Pink cubes
- Brown prisms
- Rods (coloured green and coloured alternately red and blue)
- Various geometric solids (prism, pyramid, sphere, cylinder, cone etc.)
- Rectangular tables with rough and smooth surfaces.
- A collection of various tuffs.
- Small wooden tables of different weights.
- Two boxes, each containing sixty four coloured tablets.
- A chest of drawers containing plane insets
- Three series of cards on which are pasted geometrical forms in paper.
- A collection of cylindrical closed boxes (sounds)
- A double series of musical bells, wooden boards on which are painted the lines used in music, small wooden discs for the notes

Training in following senses can be given effectively using didactic apparatus (Table)

1. Sense of touch
2. Sense of sight
3. Sense of learning
4. Sense of smooth and rough surface
5. Sense of size and shape
6. Sense of height
7. Sense of size
8. Sense of weight
9. Sense of colour
10. Sense of temperature (touch)

TABLE

Training in different senses using didactic apparatus.

	Didactic Material for providing	*Exercise in senses training*
1.	Water at Different Temperature	Presentation of water at different temperature to the child.
2.	Sand Paper roughness	Sand papers of different roughness are provided to the child and asked to touch.
3.	Small Rectangular	Board divided Into two parts, eough part and smooth part
4.	Wooden Cylinders	Child handles a series of wooden cylinders of varying heights and diameters
5.	Blocks and Rods	Variety of blocks and rods of different diameters are used for different activities.
6.	Boxes Containing Pebbles:	Exercises on boxes are provided.
7.	Blocks and Tables of different weights	Different blocks and tables that differ in weight.
8.	Wood Samples of different colours	Samples of wood of different colours. Exercises are designed on these coloured wooden samples. The

		colours are arranged and graded according to the depth of the colour.
9.	Wooden Cubes	Exercises are designed with wooden cubes. Arrangement of cubes in the vertical direction is done. Largest cube is at the base.
10.	Materials of different kinds	Exercises are based upon observations on a variety of material made of different matter (e.g., silk, wood, cotton, coarse cloth, fine cloth). Exercises are also based upon mixed materials. Students are required to separate them in pairs.
11.	Box with-six Drawers.	Each drawer has six square wooden frames.

Each frame, there is a geometrical figure in the centre. There is a small handle also. When geometrical figure is removed, child finds exactly similar form below it geometrical figures are arranged in similarity of form or shape. (circles, triangles, oval, elliptical forms, mombus etc.)

The geometrical forms are mixed and child is required to put them in right place in the drawer.

Type of sense in which training is given

1. Perception of touch is developed through the touch of water at different temperatures.
2. Perception of Touch: The sense of perception developed through the sense of touch on a variety of rough and papers.
3. Senae of different surfaces.
4. Perception of Size and Sense of Sight: Child develops the perception of size through exercises on cylinders of various heights and diameter.
5. Perception of Size and Sense of Sight: Child develops the perception of size as a result of exercises on a variety of blocks and rods.

6. Sense of Hearing: The boxes with different pebbles produce different sounds and the child develops the sense of hearing.
7. Sense of Weight: The child develops the sense of weight through different wesight exercises with blocks and tables.
8. Sense of Colour: The child develops the sense of colour as a result of a variety of exercises of coloured wood samples.
9. Sense of Height: Child develops the sense of height through Iticse simple exercises.
10. Sense of Sight and Touch: Sense of touch and sight are developed.
11. Sense of Touch, Sight, and Shape: Child develops his sense of touch sight, shape, and size.

Procedure for the use of Didactic Apparatus for Training in Senses

Didactic apparatus exercises are in line with the three psychological concepts i.e. association, recognition and recall.

1. Association: The child associates the observations making use of different senses.
2. Recognition and Distinction: The child recognises similar objects and does the required task e.g. pairing. The child finds out the difference e.g. tough surface and smooth surface ; small size or large size, less height and moreheight; low temperature or high temperature, differences in colour shades; differences in weights, differences in forms (circles, triangles, ovals, etc.)
3. Recall: The child recalls the earlier experience and solves the problem. In the given exercises.

Didactic Apparatus and Teaching of 3 Rs.

Didactic apparatus for teaching language and arithmetic is as follows :

1. Two sloping desks and various iron insets.
2. Cards on which sand paper letters are pasted.
3. Two alphabets, coloured and of different size.

4. A series of cards on which sand paper number (1, 2, 3 etc.) are pasted.
5. A series of large cards bearing same numbers on smooth paper for enumeration of numbers above ten.
6. Two boxes with small sticks.
7. The volume of drawings belonging to the method and coloured pencils.
8. The frames for lacing, buttoning etc. which are used for motor education of the hand.

Purpose for Consideration

Following points should be considered before use of didactic apparatus for teaching writing, reading and arithmetic.

1. Teaching of writing, reading and arithmetic should be taken up after training of senses.
2. Teaching of writing by teaching of reading and arithmetic. Or Montessori view the psychological principle. "Transfer of Training." ?

To quote Dr. Montessori

"Preparatory movement could be converted and reduced to a mechanism by means of repeated exercises, not on the work itself but in that which prepares font."

The above statement indicates teat sense training should follow first training in writing and then training in reading and arithmetics

Teaching of Writing : Steps

Recognition of the forms of Letters and Learning to Manipulate pencils.

1. Cut the letter alphabets in sand paper.
2. Paste the cut out letter on the cardboard.
3. Ask the child to pass his finger over the cut sum letter. This practice should be done with open eyes.
4. This will help he child to manipulate a pencil.

Learning of Sounds of Letters

1. The child is asked to trace the letter.
2. The teacher tells the relevant sound of the letter to the child.
3. The child is asked to reproduce the sound.

The above teaming of the sounds of letters, also prepare the child for reading.

Learning the Necesary Control of Pen/Pencil/Chalk.

1. The child is asked to place a metal frame on a piece of paper and draw a line around it with coloured chalk.
2. The above exercise is .repeated with a metai set instead of metal frame.

Out of the two figures (one with metal frame and the other with metal set) prepared. With the nhelp of earlier steps, the intervening figure is filled with the chalk by the child.

The child is asked to make upward and downward stokes. The child is not allowed to move their chalk or pencil outside the boundary line.

The above exercise helps the child to have a required control on the handling of the pencil/chalk/pen.

Teaching of Reading : Steps

To quote Montessori.

"Reading is the interpretation of an idea from the written signs and not merely breaking at print, Until the child receives a transmissions of ideas from the written word, he does not read."

Following steps are followed for teaching the child the skill of reading :

1. A card bearing the name of a familiar object is given to the child for reading : Geets, Ganga, Ganpati.

The utterance of the word/phrase is repeated by the child comparatively with a faster speed.

The child will come after, the places child the card under the object after successfully and correctly pronouncing the word/ phrase related to the object.

After the exercise on reading the name of the word, the child is asked to read mentally not orally, the action words/ commands written on the paper/cardboard and to perform the written action/ command.

Teaching of Arithmetic (Teaching of Addition, Substraction, Multiplication and Division): Steps

Teaching steps for arithmetic originally advocated by Dr. Montessori are not in practice put traditional procedure/steps are followed on the leading of arithmetic.

The addition, substraction multiplication and division are taught with the help of a variety of exercises making use of materials like coloured beads, numerical rods, wooden spindles, sand paper numbers, simple boxes, printed shells, long stair consisting of a set of rods of varying length (one to 10 decimeter) each rod is divided into parts painted red and blue respectively).

Training in Sense of Responsibility, Patience, Faith and Mercy.

Exercises are designed on the care of plants and animals, for the purpose of training in the sense of responsibility.

Exercises are also designed for developing patience, faith and mercy.

Teacher as Director/Directress In Mont—for! Method.

* Actually, there is no teacher in the method but the director.
* Teacher is to play the role of a guide and an director (directress) of the exercises.

To quote Montessori about education for young children;

"Conclously controlled and systematically directed."

Teacher should be familiar with the basics of child psychology.

To quote Montessori.

"The broader the teacher's scientific culture and practice in experimental psychology, The sooner will come for her the marvel of unfolding life and her interest in it. The teacher must allow full freedom to the child and not to interfere with his activity. She is simply to observe and intervene only when absolutely necessary. She is to act as a stage director in this self education process. Virtues and not words are the main qualification of the teacher. She should be partly a scientist, partly a doctor, completely religious."

Contributions of Montessori Method

Scientific Approach to education: Observation, experimentation and scientific methods of teaching were suggested.

Didactic Apparatus: Didicatics is the art/science of teaching. Didactic materials were used in a scientific way for:

— Motor training (motor education)

— Sense training (sense education)

— Teaching of writing

— Teaching of reading

— Teaching of arithmetic

— Teaching of responsibility patience, faith and mercy.

Psychological Basis of Education. The principles of child psychology were emphasised both for various exercises as well as for the understanding the nature of children (3-7 yrs.)

Individualised Instruction. Dr. Montessori emphasised on teaching of the individual teacher (Individualised instruction) she was of the opinion that every child is unique personality. Class teaching is not good. Every child needs to be observed and handled individual for proper physical and mental development.

The Child is God : Love Children.

To quote Montessori

"The child's soul which is pure and very sensitive, require our most-delicate care."

For Montassori, child is God.

Teacher Education. Montessori devoted sufficient time on the teacher education on line with her methods of teaching. Teacher education programmes were also organised in India. Dr. Montessori stayed in India from 1939 to 1951.

Teacher as Director/Directress

Teacher is to play the role of a director/directress.

Montessori School : Main Features

1. Montessori school is called "The children's House" while roebel's school is called "Children's Garden".
2. Homely atmosphere is provided in the school which is helpful in the development of the individuality of the children.
3. There are many rooms e.g.
   - — Study room
   - — Room for lunch
   - — Room for manual work
   - — Room for games and amusement
   - — Rest room

   All the rooms are properly furnished and equpped.
4. Rooms are maintained by children themselves e.g. following maintenance activities are undertaken by children themselves :
   * Cleaning the rooms
   * Dusting of the rooms
   * Laying of tables
   * Setting of the chairs
5. There is no fixed time table.
6. Class is not the unit of teaching because group teaching is not recommanded bi individual teaching is emphasised. Development of the individuality for the child is possible only through individual education.
7. Each child is free to choose his/her activities, according his/her liking/inclinations/interests.
8. A variety of exercises are provided for developing various skills/abilities/habits. e.g.
   1. Practical (Routine Skills)
   * Washing hands
   * Washing of clothes; Sweeping of rooms. Dusting of furniture

* Setting the tables and chairs
* Cleaning of nails
* Brushing the teeth
* Polishing the shoes
* Combing the hair
* Dressing and undressing manners
* Training in liberty (freedom) Performing ordinary services
* Pymnastic exercises Gymnastic

2. Motor Training : Exercises for motor training using didactic apparatus.
3. Sense Training : Sense training is giving through the use of didactic apparatus.
4. Training in writing, reading and arithmetic (training in 3 Rs).

Limitations of Montessori Method

1. Sports activities are not given importance or are neglected.
2. Much emphasis has been attached to didactic apparatus in the method.
3. Emphasis has been given to individualised instruction. Social development aspect has been neglected.
4. The activities like music, songs, drama, dance and group activities have no place. This has no place for social skill development.
5. The method is costly.
6. Teachers are not fully trained in the use of didactic apparatus. The teacher education programmes are not available or training in such schools is not upto the required standards.

Comparative Account of Montessori Method and Froebel's Playway (Kindergarten) Method

1. Similarities in Methods of Montessori & Froebel.

* Both methods are for ore-schooling of children of age group (3-7).

* Emphasis is on the self-expression and self-activity in an atmosphere of freedom.
* Individuality of the child is developed.
* Both emphasize on the love and; respect for children.
* Emphasis of self-education of children.
* Teacher should play the role in the background.
* Teacher should be guide and observer. Difference between views of Montessori and Froebet.

Montessori Method (Children's House)

1. Scientific Psychological and Practical Basis. The theory is based upon scientific; psychological and practical considerations.
2. Individualised Instruction. Instruction is for the individual. No group teaching.
3. No emphasis on social skill development and training in imagination.
4. Teaching of writing, reading and arithmetic is done with didactic apparatus.
5. Sense training with the help of didactic apparatus.
6. Emphasis on daily life activities.
7. Teacher's role is of director, guidance, observation and handling of didactic apparatus.
8. Educational method was dependent on the use of didactic apparatus. Comparatively difficult to manage.

Frobel's Playway (Kindergarten Method) (Children's Garden)

1. Metaphysical Assumptions : Educational Theory of Forbel is based upon metaphysical assumptions
2. Group Teaching : Teaching is given in group. No individual teaching.
3. Social Skill Development: Emphasis is on socialisation of the child and training in imagination. Group activities co-

operative occupations, stories, fairy tales, fables, songs, drama, poetry etc. are organised for social skills development and imagination training.

4. No teaching of writing, reading and arithmetic.
5. Sense training with the help of gift related exercises.
6. Emphasis on manual activities, e.g. clay modelling gardening. paper cutting etc.
7. Teacher's role is of a gardener and students are like tender plants.
8. Educational Method (Kindergarten) is comparatively easy. Gifts are easy to manage.

Assignments

Comment upon the following in context of John Dewey:

1. Philosophy of life
2. Education Philosophy
3. Describes various aspects of educational philosophy of John Dewey.
4. Discuss, 'Learning of dowing' in context of John Dewey.
5. Describe Forebel's philosophy of education.
6. Describe playway method with specific repference to Froebel.
7. Write briefly the principles on which Montessori method of teaching is based.
8. Discuss didactic apparatus and the Montessori method of teaching.
9. Last the main features of Montessori school. Discuss differences in the educational views of Montessori and Froebel.

7

Role of Education in Democracy

In the hands of man, Education is a useful weapon. It can work wonders if used rightly. The need of the hour is to make it society oriented. Only a good society which has definite principles and ideologies pledged to the nation can take humanity to do yeoman service in these times of crisis. Let us, therefore, revolutionize our system of education to reach the right goals without any type of wastages.

India became a democratic country with the dawn of independence. The leaders of the free country accepted democracy for the people of the country. Ever since then, efforts have been to make it a successful democratic republic. Undoubtedly, a good deal of work has been done in this direction but much more needs to be done. Then and then only we shall say that ours is a successful democratic republic.

Education is the basis with the help of which the edifice of strong democracy can be built firmly. The country has been in the grip of problems like poverty and illiteracy. And then the problem of population explosion became a big hurdle in its way of progress. Education has been used as a weapon for bringing about all round progress of the country. Due to knowledge explosion all over the globe, education is also expected to be abreast of the latest advancements in the field of science and technology. Only the use of right type of education can help really in the fast changing political and social set-up of life whose foundations are laid on democratic philosophy. So the need of the hour is to keep education upto the mark and upto date in every respect.

What is Democracy?

Let us understand the word 'democracy' in its true perspective.

The word 'democracy' is derived from two Greek words 'demos' and 'kratos' which mean 'people' and 'power', respectively. So it means the rule of the people. Democracy means, "A form of government in which the supreme power is vested in the people collectively." Abraham Lincoln said, "Democracy is government by the people, of the people and for the people." According to Seeley, "Democracy is a government in which every one has to share."

Lord Bryce said, "Democracy is the form of government in which the ruling power of the state is legally vested, not in any particular individual or class but in the members of the community as a whole." According to Radhakrishnan University Education Commission Report. "Democracy is the way of life and not a mere political arrangement. It is based on the principle of equal freedom and equal rights for all its members, regardless of race, religion, sex, occupation or economic status."

Mazzine says, "True democracy refers to the progress of all under the leadership of the wisest and the best."

Thus democracy is a way of life where we have sympathy, co-operation and the spirit of understanding. Everyone has the freedom to grow and develop as per his own potentialities. There is equality of rights and opportunities. There is liberty of thought, belief, faith and worship. It is palitical democracy.

Basic Principles of Democracy

True democracy is based on the following basic principles:

Respect for everyone. Everyone in the society has his worth and importance. In a democratic set-up of life, the dignity of an individual is held in high esteems. "Each individual is a sacred legacy of society." Democracy believes the dignity of every individual.

Freedom. 'Freedom is the soul of democracy.' Democratic set-up of life believes in the freedom of all. Every individual enjoys freedom of thought, expression, belief, faith, worship, movement and so on. Here freedom does not mean that a person may do any illegal work or do something which is anti-national. It is freedom within definite limits.

Equality of Opportunity. Every individual lives on the basis of equality. There are equal opportunities given to every one irrespective of caste, colour and creed. That way nobody has any type of grudges against anyone else.

Fellow-feelings. Everybody in the democratic society has fellow-feelings. They understand their own duties and share their feelings of oneness with the other fellows of the society. Everybody believes in mutual cooperation and the policy of give and take relationship. Democracy believes in fraternity and group living.

Toleration. The quality of toleration exists in everyone. Everybody tolerates well the leader and the other fellow-beings who are together followers of the same leader. There are healthy relationships among them all with proper toleration.

Good Citizenship: In a true democracy, every human-being happens to be a good citizen. They understand their duties and responsibilities as true citizens.

Faith in Change. Life is dynamic and so are the ways of life. Many things in life go on changing with the passage of time. A true democrat does not resist any change because he/she knows that change is natural and it may be for betterment. They always believe in co-operative living and combined efforts. Moreover, they are staunch believers of peaceful methods.

Thus democracy is a popular way of life. It is the basic philosophy of life on the basis of which our nation exists and is to make progress. Education has to be in tune with the life and philosophy of the people. Then only it is worthwhile. In the absence of a suitable type of education, the democratic society cannot exist well.

Education is the weapon of democracy and without good education for all, democracy will not be successful. Democracy without education is a contradiction in terms. The purpose of education is to ensure that human behaviour conforms to the values and ideals of democracy. Education must build the democratic convictions in the people. Democracy is a practical creed. The principles of democracy influence the theory and practice of education. They are both interdependent.

It may, however, be borne in mind that this concept of Democracy means only political democracy. In this sense, democracy is a formal structure of government through the elected representatives of people in general. This view of de.

just a misconception. To make the real concept of democracy workable and truly effective, democratic principles and values should pervade all fields of human activity, be it political, social, economic and so on. Democracy is, in fact, a way of life, a method of approach in the settlement of problem an instrument of the development of social and economic aspects of society.

Economic and social democracies are also equally important. Economic democracy means that only a few capitalists of the nation will not have the economic power in their hands. All individuals or people as a whole have that power. In other words, the production and distribution of wealth will be by the people, for the people and of the people. There is economic equality and no economic exploitation.

Social democracy abolishes all distinctions of colour, caste, creed and sex. It ensures equality of opportunities to all. Social democracy does not believe in distinction of birth, class or money. It allows maximum freedom to grow and develop to one and all. In short, justice, fair play, freedom, equality and fraternity are the watchwords of social democracy.

Thus it is clear that democracy is not a mere political deal. But it not came in gap is a way of life where community has unity in its political, economic and social aspects. Bode rightly says, "Democracy is a way of life and a way of life means a determining influence in every area of life."

Democratic Education : Its Features

Democratic type of education is needed in our country. Only then we can have successful democratic social set-up. The main features of democratic education are:

Universal and Compulsory Education. In a democratic country, education is made available to one and all. It is of universal nature and is compulsory for everybody. Such an education makes people conscious of their duties, rights and other obligations.

Free Education. Education is given free upto a certain standard. In fact, education is regarded as the birth right of every individual. Some people who are unable to receive education due to physical deformity or mental retardness are also provided with special type of education. Thus free education is provided to the blind, deaf and dumb children.

Broad-based Education. Democratic education is broad based. It has wider visions. It caters to the needs of requirements of variety of people. Thus it is found to satisfy one and all in the democratic set-up of life.

Child-centred. Democratic education is child-centred. Every child receives full attention and gets all types of facilities for his proper growth and development. Here education is provided according to the abilities and aptitudes of the child.

Community-centred. Community is the centre 'round which the whole process of education takes place. Needs and requirements of the community are well taken care of. It is related to the social environment of the community.

Provision of Adult Education. Democratic education makes provision for the education of the adults. In the society, some people fail to receive their fundamental education due to one reason or the other. It may be due to drop-outs. Democratic education provides non-formal education for such adults.

Good Citizenship. Democratic education helps in producing good citizens. It enables the Individuals to understand their duties, responsibilities and obligations towards the society and above all the nation.

De-Centralised. For giving democratic education, the environment is made fully democratic. The functioning of the institution is all decentralised. There is student's self government. The institution gives training for leadership and democratic living.

For National Unity. Democratic education keeps all the nations fully united. There may be people with different languages, different religions, different cultures but democratic type of education unites them together under the banner of democratic republic.

For International Understanding. Democratic type of education has now become the heart-felt requirement of one and all in this universe. One brotherhood, one universe, one humanity - are now fully understood by the whole humanity. Democratic education provides International understanding by developing democratic values of life.

The National Education Association of America has given 'hall-marks' of democratic education as given below:

1. Welfare of all.
2. Equal educational opportunity for all.
3. Respects the basic civil liberties.
4. Promotes economic, political and social conditions.
5. Right to determine the purposes and policies of education.
6. Favours democratic methods.
7. Efficient use of various personnels.
8. Teaches through experiences.
9. Liberates and uses intelligence of all.
10. Gives knowledge of democratic efficiency.
11. Respects humanity, tolerance, occupational efficiency and civil responsibility.
12. Promotes loyalty to democracy.

Democracy and Education

Democracy and education are inter-linked and interdependent. Democracy affects education and education affects democracy in a number of ways. Democratic principles and values have recently entered the field of education. The credit for this goes to John Dewey - the well known American educationist. According to him, "A democracy is more than a form of government, it is primarily a mode of associated living, a conjoint communicated experience." His ideas of democracy have greatly affected education. Now education has become a weapon with the help of which meaningful democracy is possible. K.G. Saiyitiain rightly said, "Education must be so oriented that it may develop basic qualities for the functioning of the democratic." Let us now study about it in details.

Democracy and Aims of Education

Democracy desires the attainment of the following aims :

(1) To make the individuals good citizens.

(2) To help everyone to become co-operative.

(3) To give training of leadership.

(4) To help in character building.

(5) To make the individuals vocationally efficient.

(6) To help everyone have good health and thus have a sound mind.

Secondary Education Commission (1952-63) has suggested the following aims of education for a democratic country.

Development of Democratic Citizenship. The success of democracy largely develops in them the qualities of (a) clear thinking (b) receptivity to new ideas (c) clearance in speech and writing, (d) the art of living in a community, (e) passion for social justice, (f) tolerance, (g) true patriotism and (h) internationalism.

Improvement of Vocational Efficiency. It includes (a) healthy attitude to work and dignity of labour, (b) technical skills and efficiency, (c) self-reliance.

Development of Personality. Democratic education is to develop the individuality of a child into a balanced and harmonious personality. Development of personality includes (a) releasing the sources of creative energy in the student, (b) cultivating rich interests (c) giving due place in the curriculum to subjects like art, craft, music, dancing, etc.

Development of the Qualities of Leadership. This is important for successful functioning of democracy. Education must train our students to shoulder the responsibility in social, political, industrial and cultural fields. Education should instil in children the readership qualities from the very beginning. Children are the future citizens and they have to assume leadership in different fields.

Development of National and International Feelings. This is very essential for the success of democracy.

The first need is development of the sense of oneness and the unity of the nation. National integration requires international understanding. No nation can exist in isolation. There is interdependence which is so essential for world peace.

Democracy and Curriculum

In a democratic country, curriculum is constructed with the purpose of realizing democratic values. Only those subjects, activities and programmes are included in the curriculum with the help in the realization of democratic values.

Democratic curriculum is organised on the basis of the following principles:

Broad-based Curriculum. Curriculum should include totality of experiences that a child receives In the class-room as well as outside the class-room. It is not just subject-centred curriculum.

Flexibility. Democratic education envisages a curriculum which is varied and flexible and satisfies the individual needs and interests. It also caters to the demands of society. Such a curriculum is not rigid. It allows necessary changes whenever situation demands or need arises thereto.

Diversified. Democratic curriculum is diversified to suit the needs of all children with different tastes, aptitude and. Intellectual background.

Related to Life, needs and Aspirations of the Pupils. The democratic approach to curriculum is based on practicalism. It is a curriculum which is directly related to the realities of life, needs and aspirations of the people. It also attends to the local needs and available resources.

Provision for Vocational Needs. It must include general 6s well as vocational aspects of eduation.....an Inter-blending of course. Democratic curriculum very well meets the needs of vocations, professional and economic requirements.

Integrated Curriculum. Democratic curriculum is constructed on the principles of integration. It is a balanced curriculum and includes different subjects, experiences and activities.

It is life-centred, activity-centred and child-centred curriculum.

Democracy and methods of Teaching

Democracy ideals and values exert a powerful influence upon the methods of teaching also. It has given birth to a number of progressive methods of teaching which are based on individual differences, learning by doing, activiity method, Dalton Plan, Heuristic Method, Experimental Method and Socialised class-room techniques.

The traditional methods are discarded. Democratic methods of teaching foster and develop the intelligence of children. Their critical reasoning has the freedom to exercise initiative and originality. Teaching and learning become a joyous experience and a shared activity.

Democracy and Discipline

Self-discipline. Democratic discipline is self-imposed. It does-not believe in repression or compulsion. It is discipline from within.

Democratic Discipline is Free Discipline. It is based on love, sympathy, co-operation, responsibility and human relationship.

Social Discipline. It develops in the pupils social attitude, habits and ideals of conduct, through the joint activities of the school which function as a community centre. Students learn self-control through social service, student's councils and social consciousness.

Democracy and Teacher

In a democratic set-up, the teacher is a friend, philosopher and guide. He holds a key position in the educative process. Every teacher is well-versed in the knowledge of his subject and he is professionally efficient.

The teacher is whole-heartedly devoted to his job and the ideals of democracy. He constitutes the environment making it congenial for the optimum development of children in terms of their talents and capacities.

The teacher in a democratic set-up has to work in close co-operation with different social groups, parents and members of the community. The purpose is to develop children as good citizens, socially oriented and dynamic members of the society.

He himself becomes a model for his students and exercises positive influence on them.

Democracy and School Administration

In democracy, school administration is based upon democratic principles and values. It is decentralised administration. It is a means to realise the goals of education i.e. to produce dynamic and productive citizens. It also works in the direction of training children in democratic living and leadership.

School administration is based on democratic spirit. It provides necessary conditions for the proper development of children's personalities. It is based on team spirit, sharing of responsibility and associated living.

It provides adequate rights and freedom to teachers in framing the school policy and programme. Teachers have their say in determining the school curriculum and methods of teaching. The school becomes a community and functions as a social organisation with democratic environment. The organisational climate is quite congenial, free and democratic in spirit.

Education for Democracy : Ways and Means

Ever since Independence, India accepted democracy and now it has not only to maintain but has also to flourish it. Plans and programmes are prepared from time to time for keeping the flame of democratic life burning successfully. Here below are suggested some ways and means which can help in a number of ways:

1. The controlling authorities of school education, the heads of the institution and the teaching personnels should plan together and then work in close collaboration with one another. That way goals will be achieved rightly without any type of wastage of energy and time and also without overlapping of efforts.

2. The curriculum for the schools should be made broad based and it should be based on the sound principles of democracy. There should be provision of diversified courses so as to give importance to individual differences and variations of attitudes and aptitudes.

3. The text-books prescribed in the school should propagate democratic values. A few chapters in the text-book may be based directly on democracy and in a few other lessons, there should be indirect preaching of democracy. This type of subject matter contained in the books will have a very good impact on the growing and developing personalities of school children.

4. The curriculum should have sufficient scope for work experience. A number of crafts may be introduced as per the requirement of the community and the locality. Thus towns having industry may introduce industry-oriented

practical work. In the case of rural school, provisions of crafts concerning agriculture may be introduced.

5. Efforts should be made to give workable knowledge of different things to the students. A few projects of work experience are repairs of watches and clocks, cycles, scooters, cars, radio, T.V., electrical appliances, wood-works, mason work etc.

6. The administration of the institution may be fully decentralised. The Head, the teachers and the students should realize that they are equally involved in the functioning of the institution.

7. Training for human relationship need be provided in the educational institutions. The students must acquire the spirit of co-operative living. The school authorities should try to set up residential schools as far as possible. It will develop fellow-feelings and co-operative living among the students. The Head of the institution and the teachers may plan together the whole teaching programme of the school. Methods such as learning the whole teaching programme of the sch ol. Methods such as learning by doing, group discussions, individualized instructions etc. should be used to the maximum in classroom teaching programme. It will develop in the students confidence and self-reliance.

8. Critical thinking should be developed in the students. This is possible if teaching is carried on by using mother tongue. It is very important at the early stages of growth and development. It is bound to hetp the students have creative thinking. Every type of creativity on the part of the students should be encouraged.

9. A few projects such as students co-operative store, student's co-operative bank, student's post office, student's canteen may be introduced in the schools with the sole purpose of imparting education to the children. It will help them to learn how they can work as a team and learn many things for their future careers.

10. Training in leadership need be given in the educational institutions. Every child has the potentialities which may be hidden but they can be recognized by the teachers.

They can be given very good training of readership. The more the leaders, the more successful will be the democracy of the country. Thus we find that educational institutions can work wonders in making the country truly democratic.

Education revives democracy, maintains democracy, refines democracy and glorifies democracy. In return thereto, democracy makes education fully democratic. Both are interlinked and interdependent. Each One helps the other to become better for the next moment. These two together make human life worth living. Surely education is very good weapon with the help of which democracy may be made all successful.

Assignments

1. Discuss in details the relationship that exists between democracy and education. Why is education for true democracy very essential for our country today ?
2. If we accept the attainment of democracy as our ultimate goal, what policies and practices must be followed in our schools ?
3. Liberty and equality are two great principles of democracy. How can we promote them through education ?
4. There is a functional relationship between democracy and education. Bring out the relationship between the two and discuss the important ways and means of achieving this relationship.
5. "If democracy is to be stable form of government of a country, education for democracy must be introduced and maintained at all costs." Discuss the statement briefly.
6. How can education for democracy be imparted successfully in the present day situations prevailing in the schools?
7. What do you understand by democratic conception of education ? Discuss briefly the views about curriculum, methods, teacher and discipline of the democratic education.
8. Discuss the importance of 'Education for Democracy' keeping in view the democratic set-up of our country.

8

Role of Education in Socialism

Equality and Equity in society are the constitutional provisions in India. Socialism has been viewed variously. In India, method of socialism are based upon parliamentary democracy using gradualist evolutionary processes. Goals of education in India in relation to socialism have been determined taking into consideration Indian democratic system and problems of Indian society. The present chapter deals briefly, the meaning of socialism, sociology, goals of socialism, goals of socialism in relation to education, problems in the development of egalitarian Indian social order through education, meaning and importance of sociology of education, role of education in achieving goals of socialism and programmes for achieving goals of socialism.

Meaning of Socialism

According to Webster's Comprehensive Dictionary, meaning of the concept socialism in different contexts is reproduced here to pick up the meaning with specific reference to meaning of the concept socialism in terms of Indian Socialistic Republic:

1. Public collective ownership or control of the basic means of production, distribution, and exchange, with the avowed aim of operating for use rather than for profit, and of assuring to each member of society an equitable share of goods, services, and welfare benefits; as a system of social and economic organisation planned, attempted or achieved through various methods for examples

Methods in Utopian or Christian Socialism: Methods involve cooperative communal groups holding all things in common.

Methods in Guild socialism: Methods based upon organisation of producer groups and the professions in syndicalist guilds to be represented in a federal legislative body.

Methods in Fabian or British Labour Party Socialism: Methods are based upon parliamentary democracy using gradualist evolutionary processes.

Methods in Marxist-Leninist State Socialism: Methods are based upon revolution, expropriation, and dictatorship of the so called proletariat, in short, communism.

Creeping Socialism: Methods are based upon anything considered as a gradual or piecemeal encroachment upon the system of private property and free enterprise through state action: used as an epithet.

Meaning of Sociology

1. Webster's Comprehensive Dictionary: Sociology is the science that treats of the origin and evaluation of human society and social phenomenon, the progress of civilization and the laws controlling institutions and functions.
2. Auguste Comte a French philosopher, used the word "Sociology in 1837. He used this word to designate the application of the scientific method to the study of human nature and society. According to Comte, Sociology is a fundamental science because it had a method of exact investigation. Comte placed Sociology in the hierarchy of sciences at the end: Mathematics, Astronomy, Physics, Chemistry, Biology, Psychology and Sociology. Comte held that Sociology dealt with social phenomena, which he thought, were complex and difficult to describe.
3. Frederic Le play a contemporary of Comte followed scientific and objective approach to the study of social problems.
4. Herbert Spencer published his book entitled "Principles of Sociology" in 1876. He considered that human individual was like a cell and society was like an organism. Individuals perform different functions as cells in the organism perform different functions. Cells function in relation to other cells and the total organism. Similarly, individuals function in

relations to other individuals and total society. Individuals in advanced societies are more differentiated as compared to those of less advanced societies.

5. Moore and Cole considered sociology as the study of plural behaviour. Plural behaviour is the behaviour in relation to others - the behaviour of man in relation to other men and in relation to the groups or associations. Sociar interaction is the central theme of sociology. It includes the interaction with culture and other institutionalised interaction patterns such as the family, the play group, religions, economic and educational institutions i.e. every form of group living.
6. **Duncan:** The scientific study of the processes of interactions of persons and the patterns these form in relation to biological, psychological and cultural influences. The views of Duncan highlight that interactions are influenced by biological, psychological and cultural Factors.
7. **Merril and Eldridge:** Sociology is the study of human relationships. The studies include the way human beings interact with other human beings; study of customs and traditions that grow out of these interactions; study of institutions that crystallise these basic human interests and the change that occur in these institutions; study of changes in the light of human welfare; study on the effects of changes on the behaviour and personality development of the individual.
8. **Ginsberg:** Sociology is the study of society, that is, of the web or tissue of human interaction and interrelations. Sociology may also be defined as study of human interactions and interrelations, their conditions and consequences.
9. **Robbins:** Sociology deals with the whole man in relation to all the social, cultural and bio-physical backgrounds. Sociology studies man in his total social relationship which include all aspects such as political, economic, psychological, religious, etc. The main focus is on social relationship. Sociology studies culture, religions and other institutions as these throw light on social relationships.
10. **Alex Inkles:** Sociology is the study of social order which is the underlying regularity of human social behaviour.

11. **Max-Weber:** Sociology is a science which interprets social behaviour with the aim of arriving at causal explanation of human behaviour.

Scope of Sociology

1. Sociology explains inter-personal and group behaviour. Every individual is a member of a group by birth or choice. Groups play a continuous and effective roles in developing the personality of an individual and at—explains the causes of the behaviour of the individual.
2. Sociology explains nature of social groups such as the family, the community, the occupational groups, religious groups, racial groups, and the notion of the state.
3. Sociology explains various social changes that are taking place within a group life.
4. Sociology explains various processes of interaction (competition, conflict, co-operation, accomodation and assimilation) and their results such as acculturation and socialisation.
5. Sociology studies social change and social control.
6. Sociology studies the concepts of civilization and culture.
7. Sociology studies social problems such as crime, juvenile delinquency, poverty and their possible solutions.

Goals of Socialism

To quote Preamble of Indian Constitution;

"We, the people of India, having solemnly resolved to constitute India into a sovereign, democratic and socialist republic and to secure to all its citizens Justice (social, economical and political), liberty of thought, expression, belief and worship, and equality of status and opportunity and to promote among them all fraternity assuring the dignity of the individual and unity of the nation."

To quote Indian Constitution:

"The development of India as a great cooperative common wealth necessarily meant equality of opportunity and social justice for all. Any narrow communalism or provincialism must, therefore, be repressed and the evil of the caste rooted out."

The constitution's provisions are for the development of egalitarian Indian social order. Education is an instrument to achieve these constitutional provisions.

According to Dr. M.S. Sachdeva, characteristics of socialistic pattern of Indian society are as follows:

1. Principal means of production in the Indian society should be under the social ownership of control.
2. Rate of production should increase through required steps.
3. The national wealth should be distributed equally i.e. principle of equality in distribution should be followed.

Goals of Socialism in Relation to Education

1. Provision of universal education.
2. Equality in educational opportunity.
3. Spelling out the social aim of education in line of spirit of socialistic pattern in India or social skills development.
4. Curriculum development for social development of Indian citizens.
5. Strategies of teaching for development of social skills in the learners; Examples: Socialised recitation methods Project method Team teaching. Large group teaching techniques e.g. seminar, conference, panel discussion etc.
6. Discipline concept and socialism

Problems in the Development of Egalitarian Indian Social Order

1. Sex	2. Colour	3. Race
4. Language	5. Caste	6. Religion
7. Politicial opinion	8. Social origin	9. Economic condition
10. Birth	11. Illiteracy	12. Poverty

13. Unemployment

14. No emphasis on national unity.

All the above factors have no place in the concept of equality and equity in education. Education can help to tackle these problems and developing egalitarian Indian social order.

Meaning and Importance

Meaning. Sociology of education is an analysis of sociological processes involved in the educational institutions. This area of study has evolved out of the field of Educational Sociology which is defined as the application of general principles and findings of sociology to the administration and for process of education.

According to Vipula Chaturvedi (quoted by Pandey 1983), Sociology of Education is concerned with educational aims, methods, institutions, curricula and administration in relation to political, religious, social and cultural forces of society. It endeavours to examine the influence of social life and social relationship on the development of personality of an individual.

According to Ottaway, Sociology of Education focusses upon the social relations by which the individual gains experiences.

Importance.

1. The aims of education are determined in the context of development of social behaviour of the learners.
2. Curricula are developed according to social aims of education. These serve as means with the help of which social behaviour of individuals can be developed.
3. Methods of teaching are determined in line with social aims and curricula.
4. Social discipline can be developed among individual. Individuals behave in a manner keeping in view the interests of other people also. Individual interests are not only taken into consideration.
5. Educational institutions are considered as social system or a sub-social system of the social system. Such concept of the educational institution helps in the development of desirable social behaviour in an individual.
6. The teacher education programmes (aims, curricula, methods, institutions) should be oriented in the light of development of social behaviours among teachers so that they may play their roles for bringing desirable social values and attitudes among students.
7. Educational administrators are oriented in the light of social aims of education.

Role of Education in Achieving Goals of Socialism

Aims of Education: Studies are done regarding determination of social aims with the changing times.

Curriculum: Studies on development of curricula are based upon sociological principles with the changing times.

Methods of Teaching: Methods of teaching are identified for development of desirable social behaviour of learners. Project method, problem-solving methods, small group methods (seminar, workshop, etc.) are already in use for achieving desired social aims.

Learning Resources: Studies on the programmes and provision of learning resources are done in line with social aims of education.

Teacher Education: Studies on teacher education programmes and educational administrators/managers are done in light of social aims of education.

Factors of Social change: Studies on the influence of forces (political, religious, social and cultural) are done that influence the social life and social relationship of every individual or a group of individuals.

Education as Instrument of Social Change: Studies are being done on the role of education as an instrument of socialisation.

Transmission of values: Studies on the role of education as a means of transmission of cutlural values are being carried out.

Social Change: Studies on the role of education for bringing desirable social change by bringing change in the attitude and value system of learners.

Educational Programmes and Egalitarian Indian Social Order

1. Common School System.
2. Neighbourhood schools.
3. Navodaya Vidyalayas.
4. Universalisation of primary education.
5. Formal and non-formal programmes for secondary education.

6. Women education at all levels of education: primary, secondary and tertiary.
7. Education of scheduled castes and tribes at all levels.
8. Education of the handicapped, Physical & Mental.
9. Adult education for all sections at all levels of education.
10. Distance education for all citizens at all levels of education.
11. Sanskritisation & Westernisation and modernisation strategies for social development.

Assignments

1. Discuss the meaning and scope of Sociology.
2. Comment upon the following:
   (a) Varied views on the concept of Sociology.
   (b) Scope of Sociology.
   (c) Auguste Comte and Sociology.
3. Give a comparative account of meaning and scope of Sociology and Sociology of Education.
4. What do you mean by Sociology of Education. Discuss its need, importance and scope.
5. Define Sociology of Education. Write about its scope.
6. Give a comparative account of Sociology and Sociology of Education.
7. Comment upon the following:
   (a) Meaning of Sociology and Sociology of Education.
   (b) Scope of Sociology and Sociology of Education.

9

Role of Education in Secularism

Education for Secularism

Ever since India got freedom in 1947, the word 'secular' has been used very often by the national leaders. Every one says, "India is a secular-country." In every political and educational corner, secularism is being propagated. Let us now acquaint ourselves with the word 'secular'. The word 'secular' has been derived from the Latin word "Seculum" which means 'age' or 'generation'.

The term 'secularism' was first used by George Jacob Holydake in the nineteenth century. He used this word in the context of social and ethical values. According to Holydake, the concept of socialism may be defined as a system, "which seeks the development of physical, moral and intellectual nature of man to the highest possible point as the immediate duty of life which inculcates the practical sufficiency of natural morality apart from Atheism, Theism or Bible which selects as its methods of procedure of promotion of human improvement by material means."

As per Oxford Dictionary, the word secular means sceptical of religious truth, opposed to religious education. It does not mean irreligion or anti-religion or irreligiousness. In fact, the word secularism shows our broad mindedness.

Bradlaugh, a successor of Holydake says, "Secularism is hostile to religion."

According to Chambers Dictionary "secularism is, the belief that the state morals, education etc. should be independent of religion."

Webster's Dictionary states that secularism is, "the belief that religion and ecclesiastical affairs should not enter into the functions of the state." Webster further says, "A system of doctrines and practices that rejects any form of religious faith and worship."

The pluralistic view is that secularism is an attitude of accepting all religions rather than rejecting any or all religions. This view was put forth by Mahatma Gandhi and Dr. S. Radhakrishnan.

Mahatma Gandhi put forth his view, "The soul of religion is one but it is encashed in a multitude of forms. Wise men will ignore the outward crust and see the same soul living under a variety of crusts." Then in 1928 he said, "After long study and experience, I have come to the conclusion that

(1) All religions are true.

(2) All religions have some errors in them.

(3) All religions are almost as dear to me as my own Hinduism.My veneration for other faiths is the same as to my own faith."

In this context Dr. S. Radhakrishnan says, "Secularism does not mean anything irreligious or atheism or even stress on material comforts. Rather it lays stress on the universality of spiritual values which may be attained by a variety of ways."

There is establishment of a secular polity. Every religion is important and so every religion should be respected. All religions basically have the same beliefs and ultimately advocate to reach the same goals. There is need of imbibing qualities like tolerance, co-operation and understanding. There should be no place for religious prejudices. According to Mahatma Gandhi, "My veneration for other faiths is the same as for my own faith." "We believe in Sarva-Dharma-Samantar-having equal regard for all faiths and creeds."

Regarding the secular state, Donald E. Smith says, "A state which guarantees individual and co-operative freedom of religion, deals with the individual as a citizen irrespective of his religions, is not constitutionally connected to a particular religion nor does it seek either to promote or interfere with religion."

Dr. B.R. Ambedkar explained the concept of secular state, "All that a secular state means is that this parliament shall not be competent to impose any particular religion upon the rest of the people."

Present Situation in India

India is a multi religious and culturally varied society. People have different religions and they have different beliefs. A large number of people is uneducated. That is why, people have narrow mindedness. Value crises have also deteriorated the social set up of life. Fanaticism and communalism are on the increase. During the recent past, people started believing in regionalism. Ram Janam Bhumi and Babri Masjid became the issues of great struggle between the different communities. In this type of prevailing situations, there is great need of educating the people on the right lines. That way only selfishness and narrow mindedness of the people can be ended. And they can be made to realize the importance of national unity and emotional integrity.

There is need of making the people open minded. Only a broad minded person is able to make adjustment in any and every type of situation. Equality, liberty, fraternity, national outlook and international understanding need be propagated. Moral values have to be imbibed. Scientific attitude in order to have rationality and objectivity need be developed in the fast growing and developing generations.

In the present set up of life where there is erosion of values, narrow mindedness and selfishness spreading, trifles over petty religious matters are caused. Corruption and disbelief are rampant. How can all this be improved? Who can be entrusted with the job of shouldering the whole responsibility? The only suitable weapon for this is Education. In the words of D.E. Smith, "Secularism's best hope for future in India lies in its class-rooms."

Secondary Education Commission says, "The educational system must make its contribution to the development of habit, attitude and qualities of character which will enable its citizens to counteract all those fissiparous tendencies which hinder the emergence of a broad, national and secular outlook."

The National Policy on Education (1986) says, "In our culturally plural society, education should fo'ster universal and eternal values, oriented towards the unity and integration of our people. Such value education should help eliminate obscurantism, religious fanaticism, violence, superstition and fatalism."

Major Recommendation of Commissions

Major recommendations of different commissions are as under :—

University Education Commission (1948)

1. That all educational institutions start work with a few minutes for silent meditation.
2. That in the first year of degree course, lives of great religious leaders like Gautam, the Buddha, Confucious, Zoroaster, Socrates, Jesus, Sankara, Ramanujan, Mohammad, Kabir, Nanak, Gandhi be taught.
3. That in the second year some selections of a universal character from the scriptures of the world be studied.
4. That in the third year, the central problem of the philosophy of religion be considered.

Secondary Education Commission (1953)

The Commission is of the view that "He;.'thy trends in regard to religious or moral behaviour spring from three sources:

1. The influence of the home which is the dominant factor.
2. The influence of the school through the conduct and beraviour of the teachers themselves and life in the school community as a whole.
3. Influence exercised by the public of the locality and the extent to which public opinion prevails in all matters pertaining to religious instruction or moral instruction, the Commission has recommended.

"One of the methods adopted in some schools is to hold assembly at the commencement of the day's session with teachers and pupils present, when a general non-donominational prayer is offered. Moral instruction in the sense of inspiring talks given by suitable persons selected by the headmaster and dwelling on the lives of great personages of all times and of all climes will help to drive home the lesson of morality. In view of the provision of the constitution of the secular state, religious instructions cannot be given in schools except on voluntary basis and outside the regular school hours; such instructions should be given to the children of the particular faith and with the consent of the parents and the management concerned.

Sri Prakasa Committee (1959)

Sri Prakasa Committee, 1959, constituted for this purpose, gave the following suggestions:

Elementary Stage

1. The School Assembly should be held for a few minutes in the morning for group singing.
2. Simple and interesting stories about the lives and teachings of prophets, saints and religious leaders should be included in the syllabus for language teaching.
3. Audio-visual material connected with the main living religions of the world should be included especially in the teaching of Geography.
4. In the school programme, two periods a week should be set aside for moral instruction. Dogmas and rituals should be excluded from moral instruction. Kothari Education Commission has also made similar recommendations.
5. Physical education and all forms of play in the school should contribute to the building of character and the inculcation of the spirit of true sportsmanship.

Secondary Stage

1. The Morning Assembly should observe two minutes's silence followed by readings from the scriptures and classics. Community singing should also be encouraged.
2. The essential teachings of the great world religions should be studied as part of the curriculum pertaining to Social Studies and History. Simple texts and stories concerning different religions may be included in the syllabus.
3. One hour a week should be assigned to moral instruction. Suitable speakers may be invited.
4. Organised social service during holidays and outside class hours should be an essential part of school programme. This is very helpful in teaching the dignity of manual

labour, love of humanity, patriotism and self-discipline. Participation in games and sports should be compulsory and physical education including sex education, should form a normal part of school programme.

5. Qualities of character and behaviour of students should form an essential part of the overall assessment of a student's performance at school.

University Stage

(a) Silent meditation should be encouraged.

(b) General study of different religions should be an essential part of the general education course in degree classes. In this connection, the recommendations made by the University Education Commission should also be incorporated.

(c) A Course in Comparative Religions may be introduced. In other words, there should be University Department in the comparative study of religion.

(d) A fairly long period of social service should be introduced by all universities.

Views of National Policy on Education (1986)

Change in Curriculum: The growing concern over the erosion of essential values and an increasing cynicism in society has brought to focus the need for re-adjustments in the curricultum in order to make education a forceful tool for the cultivation of social and moral values.

Universal and Eternal Values: In our culturally plural society, education should foster universal and eternal values, oriented towards the unity and integration of our people. Such value education should help eliminate obscurantism, religious fanaticism, violence, superstition and fatalism.

Positive Content: A part from this combative role, value education has a profound positive content, based on our heritage, national goals and universal perceptions. It should lay primary emphasis on this aspect.

Views of Programme of Action (1986)

The "Programme of Action" which is the follow up measure

to National Policy of Education, has laid down some concrete steps to achieve the desired goals as stated below:

"A special place has been assigned to imparting of value oriented education in the Education Policy document. A beginning would be made by instituting a special study value-oriented education. Based on its analysis, it would in collaboration with NCERT and State institutions, help in suggesting broad parameters of values of integrity, truth, devotion, loyalty etc. with particular reference to their embodiment in Indian heritage so as to blend naturally with the over-all educational process."

Naturally then the authorities concerned with education will have to work vigorously to achieve the desired ends. Now let us see what can be possible at the hands of different authorities concerned with education.

Administrative and Controlling Authorities

The controlling authorities of education can play a vital role as suggested below:

1. Universal compulsory and free education for all upto 14 years of age has been the slogan of the government ever since India got freedom. Good many efforts have been made for this but the overall achievement is much below the desired targets. The obvious reason being poverty stricken ever growing population. There is need of making provision of part time education facilities. Special type of education need be provided to the children of this category which should help them to earn sufficiently along side their learning. There is need of introducing practical oriented education, work based education which would enable the learner to become proficient in some vocation or job. When the children will learn by working with their hands, they will become an asset to their families as well as to the community and the nation they belong to.

2. Suitable type of curriculum should be prescribed in the schools. The different activities and the textbooks should propagate the chief characteristics of secularism. Different lessons in the books should reflect love and respect for all religions.

3. The authorities can introduce moral education as a compulsory paper for all the students. It will change the

outlook of the students. They will have good qualities like honesty, sincerity, hardwork, fellow-feeling, co-existence, non-violence etc

4. Efforts can be made to introduce a subject like 'Comparative Religions Study'. Efforts should be made to popularize this subject in the senior classes. Of course for juniors there may be elementary type of study of different religions. For example in the lower classes, the textbook on this subject may consist of biographies of founders of some popular religions.

5. Newspapers and journals can play a leading part in propagating the characteristics of secularism. Some journals may be selected which can educate the masses. The newspa-pers may also have, one page per week, totally based on secular education. The intellectuals may be asked to write their articles for the newspapers and also for the journals.

6. Radio and T.V can also be used to educate the public fully about secularism. The Public Relation Officers (PROs) at district headquarters can use T.V. and Radio for the achievement of goals.

Role of Teachers and Headmasters

In the schools, the teachers and the headmasters can play significant roles. No doubt, the higher authorities can prescribe certain things but it is the teachers community that can actually put those things in practical shape. Without their whole hearted co-operation nothing in this regard can be achieved. Now let us see how the schools can help in imparting secular based education:

1. **Moral Education, Religious Education, Comparative Religious Studies.** All these subjects should be entrusted to the matured teachers. In the hands of such teachers, there will be no misunderstanding and no basic mis-representation of facts and figures. The personalities of such teachers in themselves will be good examples for the students to follow.

2. **Every school should celebrate religious festivals pertaining to different religions.** At least one function of

each religion must be celebrated in the institution. Efforts should be made that festivals of all religions should be celebrated with equal pomp and show. In the celebration of each such function, students belonging to different religions should be associated. The school authorities should ensure that all religious festivals are given equal importance.

3. The school authorities should organise declamation contests on topics related to all religions. While doing so, it must be ascertained that nothing happens which injures'the feelings of one religious group or the other. There should be some internal checking of the material being presented by the students in the gathering. The teachers incharge of declamation contest should make all efforts to maintain that the central string of all religions is one.

4. Extension lectures on topics of comparative religious study may be organised in the schools. Eminent scholars of different religions may be invited for giving lectures to the students. Only those persons should be invited who have made comparative study of different religions.

5. In the institutions, tours and trips may be organised. The students may be taken to different centres of religions. Thus the students may be taken to see 'Guru Gobind Singh Bhawan' in the Punjabi University, Patiala. The very sight of the building, showing the studies of different religions and all ultimately uniting and showing oneness will have deep impact on the personalities of the children. Just possible some students may take up comparative religious studies for their post-graduate degree.

6. In different religions, many things are common such as social service at the time of celebrations, service to humanity etc. may be highlighted in the schools. The students may be encouraged to take up such activities. Once the dignity of social service is realized by the students, it has then everlasting impact on their personalities.

7. The institutions should lay greater emphasis upon teaching religious studies through informal type of instructions. The students can be encouraged to think of points common

in different religions. Those thoughts/ideas may be highlighted in the morning assembly or at some other occasion when there is a gathering.

No doubt, our country is secular and we are expected to believe in secularism. For this we shall have to make efforts in different ways. Only then people will become fully conscious of it and the goals behind would be achieved. Both formal and informal ways need be applied for it. Education can certainly deliver the goods if it is planned with those motives in mind.

Assignments

1. What is secularism? Discuss the need and importance of secular based education.
2. What are the characteristics of a secular state? How is our educational system trying to create a social climate in the country in which secular values are sought to be promoted?
3. Write short notes on:

   (a) Secular based Education.

   (b) Secularism and Education.

10

Education and Culture Development

Culture of every social order is unique. Culture has material and non-material aspects. Material aspects are the material object which we use in our day to day life. Non-material aspects are the value system, attitudes, opinions, beleifs etc. Education is an instrument that helps us to preserve and transmit the required aspects of culture. New aspects (both material as well as non-material ones) are also transmitted taking into consideration present and future needs if the society). Thus, there is a positive correlation between culture and education. Present Chapter deals certain aspects of culture and its relationship with education.

Concept of Culture

The word "culture" has been derived from a Latin word "culture" which means to "to cultivate." A few definitions are mentioned below:

1. Cuber: Culture, in terms of anthropology, is a continually changing pattern of learned behaviour and the products of the learned behaviour including attitudes, values, knowledge and material objects are shared by and transmitted among the members of society.
2. Arnold Mathew: The best that has been thought and known is culture. Culture includes the ways of life, the habits, the manners, the very tones of voices, the literature, the things which give pleasure to the community, the words, the thoughts, which make the furniture of their minds.
3. Ottaway: The culture of a society means the total way of life of a society.

4. Taylor: Culture is that complex whole, which includes knowledge, belief, art, morals, law, custom and any other capabilities and habits acquired by man as member of society.
5. Brown: Culture is the total behaviour pattern of the group conditioned in part by the physical environment, both natural and man made, but primarily by the ideas, attitudes, values and habits which have been developed by the group to meet the needs.
6. Rugg: Culture means the total life of the people that goes on with these groups; what the people in a given society do, think, feel, behave, desire, fear, etc.
7. Maclver and Page: Culture is the realm of styles, of values, of emotional attachments, of intellectual adventures. Culture, then is the antithesis of civilizaton. It is the expression of our nature in our modes of living and our thinking, intercourse, in our literature, in religion, in recreation and efoyment.
8. Ellwood: Culture includes on the one hand the whole of man's material civilization, tools, weapons, system of industry, and on the other hand, all the non-material or spiritual civilization such as language, literature, art, religion, morality, law and government.
9. Sutherland and Woodland: Culture includes anything that can be communicated from one generation to another. The culture of the people is their social heritage, a complex whole, which includes knowledge, belief, art, morals, laws, techniques of food, fabrication and use, and modes of communication.
10. K.M. Munshi: Culture is the characteristic way of life inspired by fundamental values in which people live.
11. Swami Dayanand: Culture consists of the acceptance of truth and abandonment of untruth.
12. Gandhi: Culture is the foundation, the primary thing. It should show itself in the smallest detail of your conduct and personal behaviour.
13. Nehru: Culture is the widening of the mind and of the spirit.

Characteristics

1. Culture is a learned quality.
2. Culture is transmitted from person to person and generation to generation.
3. Culture is social but not the individual heritage.
4. Culture is idealistic. It stands for ideals and norms for human behaviour.
5. Culture meets and satisfies the social and ethical needs of man. Thus culture has the gratifying quality.
6. Each culture tries to adopt the qualities outside its own environment. The contact of two or more cultures takes place and the interaction of two cultures leads to adaptation. Thus culture has the adaptive quality.
7. Different aspects of culture have the integrative quality.
8. Culture is in a constant flux i.e.it is always in the process of change. Culture changes as the society changes. Thus culture is dynamic in quality.
9. Culture is the manifestation of man's mind in varying moods of nature and environment and in the changing course of history.

Material and Non-Material Dimensions of Culture

Material Dimension of Culture

Material dimension of culture includes material aspects e.g.:-

1. Materials that contribute to better standard of living.
2. Materials that contribute to development of natural resources, human capital and technological resources.
3. Materials that contribute to control population problem.
4. Materials that contribute to control environmental problem.

Non-material Dimension of Culture

Aspects of non-material dimension of culture are human. Ideas, interests, appreciations, opinions, attitudes and values. The change in ideas and values is affected by a series of factors.

Specific examples:

1. Positive attitude for national and economic development of India.
2. Positive attitude for vocational and technical education.
3. Positive attitudes for savings.
4. Positive attitudes for small family norms.
5. Positive attitudes for improving standard of living.
6. Positive attitude for inter-cultural activities.
7. Values related to nationalism.
8. Values related to internationalism.
9. Values related to democracy.
10. Values related to socialism.
11. Values related to secularism (respect for every religion).
12. Values related to egalitarian society.
13. Values of co-operation and interdependence.
14. Social and cultural values related to industrialisation, modernisation and technological advancement.
15. Positive attitudes and values for maintaining healthy environment.
16. Scientific attitudes, scientific temper and rationality.
17. Respect for innovation, cultural diffusion and integration of new ideas.
18. Positive attitudes and values for conservation of natural resources.
19. Respect and tolerance for various ideologies or view points.
20. Appreciation for social-cultural problems and appropriate aparticipation towards their effective solution.
21. Tolerance for diversified socio-cultural values.
22. Respect for Indian Constitution.
23. Respect for law and order.

24. To feel proud of to be an Indian and buy Indian materials of consumption.
25. Respect for the process of Sanskritisation and Westernisation.

Relationship between Culture and Education

There are two ways to discuss relationship between culture and education. The relationship can be discussed under the following two sub-headings.:

1. Functions of education towards culture.
2. Functions of culture towards education.

Functions of Education Towards Culture

Education influences culture in the following ways:

1. Preservation of cultural heritage.
2. Transmission of culture.
3. Development/promotion of culture.
4. New cultural patterns.
5. Maintaining continuity of culture.
6. Removing cultural lag.

Conservation and Preservation of Cultural Heritage. Education helps in the conservation and preservation of cultural heritage. The conservative function of education has been emphasized by many authorities e.g. Percy Nunn, Dr. Radhakrishnan, Pandit Nehru, etc. According to Percy Nunn, special functions of education are to: (a) consolidate nation's spiritual strength; b) maintain nation's historic continuity; (c) secure nation's past achievements; and to (d) guarantee nation's future.

According to Pandit Nehru, education must help in preserving the vital elements of our heritage. The core of India's cultural heritage is love of beauty and truth, spirit of tolerance, capacity to absorb other cultures and work out new synthesis.

Transmission of Culture. Education helps in the transmission of cultural patterns, traditions, experience, values and norms. There is no growth and development of man without transmission of culture, the chaos in the society may be there in case the transmission of culture is not done properly. Traditions may be destroyed which may cause the breaking of the society into pieces. This situation may lead to loss of values, truth, justice, ideals and that may lead to socially undesirable behaviours of individuals. This situation is harmful to the society. Education saves us from his situation. According to Ottaway, "one of the tasks of education is to hand-over the cultural values and behaviour patterns of the society to its young and potential members".

Development of Culture. Education causes the development of culture. A better and more developed society is formed through education. According to D.J.O. Connon, "If each generation had to learn for itself, what has been learned by its predecessors, no sort of intellectual or social development would be possible and the present state of society would be little different from the society of the old stone age." Education provides experiences that reorganize and restructure human experiences and as a result of this human culture and civilization develops.

Development of New Cultural Patterns and Adjustment with these Cultural Patterns. New cultural patterns are developed with the help of education as an instrument of social change. New knowledge, values, skills are generated through education which modify the behaviour of individuals. Education helps individuals in making adjustment with new cultural patterns.

Maintaining Continuity of Culture. Culture is the life blood of a society. Without culture, a society is bound to decay and die sooner or later Education upholds the continuity of culture through its diverse activities and programmes. The continuity of cultural condition is an essential condition for the survival of a nation.

Removing Cultural Lag. Due to certain type of crisis, lack of adjustment and constraints, the progress of culture comes to halt or there is a cultural crisis. This results into cultural lag. Similarly, when material culture develops at a fast pace due to scientific and technological developments, non-material culture consisting of ideals, values and norms lag behind. There is no harmony between the two components (material and non-material) of culture. There is a clash of values as well as of ideologies. Education is the only means to bridge this cultural lag by its activities and programmes of development.

Influences of Culture

Cultural components, material and non-material influence the education which is considered as a social process or activity in a society. Educational aspects which are influenced by culture are briefly described below:

1. Aims of Education: Aims of education are determined taking into consideration the culture of the society.
2. Curriculum Development: Aims provide the guidelines for the development of instructional material to be followed in the educational institutions for the purpose of achieving desirable social aims.
3. Methods of Teaching: Culture helps in choice of appropriate methods of teaching to achieve aims.
4. Development of Social Disicipline. Culture determines the nature of social discipline to be developed in an individual with the help of educational system.
5. Teacher and Teacher Education Programmes. Culture is the base for taking decisions regarding the roles of pre-service and in-service teachers in educational institutions.
6. Educational Environment in Educational Institutions: Cultural patterns, values, beliefs determine social environments in educational institutions.

Values, Traditions and Religion : Meaning and Importance

Meaning of Values

A few definitions of values are listed below:

1. Kluckhohn: Value is a conception, explicit or implicit, distinctive of an individual or characteristic of a group, of the desirable which influences the selection from available means and ends of action.
2. R.K. Mukherjee: Values are socially approved drives and goals that are internalised through the process of conditioning, learning or socialization, and that becomes subjective preferences, standards and aspirations.
3. Parker: Values belong wholly to the inner world of mind. The satisfaction of desire is the real value, the thing that

serves is only an instrument. A value is always an experience, never a thing or an object.

4. R.B. Perry. Any objective whatever it be, acquires values when any interest, whatever it be, is taken in it, just as anything whatsoever becomes a target when anyone whosoever aims at it.
5. E. Brightman: In the most elementary sense, value means whatever is actually liked, prized, esteemed, desired, approved, or enjoyed at any time. It is the actual experience of enjoying a desired object or activity.
6. John Dewey: The term "value" has two quite different meanings. On the one hand, it denotes the attitude of prizing thing, finding it worthwhile, for its own sake or intrinsically. So, value in this sense is to appreciate but to value also means a distinctly intellectual act, an operation of comparing and judging to evaluate.
7. Prem Kripal: Values may be defind as:

   (a) What we believe (professed values);

   (b) What we practice (operational values); and

   (c) What we learn from experience.

In order to adopt and renew traditions received from the past traditional values, he further remarks, "Values should be operational and also relevant and dynamic. Values should not be crystallized and frozen to the point of rigidity, stopping further growth and renewal."

Importance of Values

Values and Growth and Development of an Individual and Society. Different types of values (biological, economic, affecting, social, intellectual, aesthetic, moral, religious, etc.) affect the growth and development of an individual and the society. In the absence of moral, social, cultural, economic values, man stands zeroed and is considered insignificant. Society whose individuals have lost values is called poor and backward society.

Erosion of values is seen at all levels leading to spread of greed, injustice, insensitivity, and what not. Dr. Sampooran Singh writes on the erosion of social values in India, "Thoughts, ideologics, codes of conduct and sets of values, psychological pattern of behaviour have failed in transforming man. Man with the help of thought organisation has created a marvellous scientific and technological world, but human being, as an individual is unhappy and frustrated, not at peace with himself, not at harmony with different layers of his being."

Values and Sub-systems of the Society. Subsystems of the society (political, economic, educational, social, industrial, religious systems) depend upon values, e.g.

1. Political values affect everyone. We, in India and the world over, observe a decline in value system at political level. There is a need to check the erosion of values at this level and it is affecting at other levels also.
2. Economy also depends upon values of individuals.
3. Growth and development of industry depends upon values.
4. Religious values affect people's opinion and behaviour.

Values and Educational Institutions. The environment in different educational institutions depends upon value systems being followed. Decline in value systems leads to decline in educational standards. We see the effects of declining values in our schools, colleges and university. We have to follow values that may contribute to proper functioning of our educational institutions.

Values and Family. Family, peaceful environment and its development depend upon value system followed in a particular family. We generally find that disputes are there among family members. This is due to erosion of values. Respect for each other in the family is generally lacking. Cooperation, sympathy etc. are generally declining.

Values and Neighbourhood/Locality. Behaviour of individuals at a particular locality depends upon their values. We generally observe that people are least concerned with each other in the neighbour in big cities (in towns and villages, the feelings and values are different).

Traditions: Meaning and Importance

Meaning of Tradition

1. Traditions are unwritten body of beliefs, facts, etc. handed down importance to generation.
2. Traditions are the custom, or practice of long standing.

Importance of Tradition

Conservation of Relevant Traditions: There are certain traditions which are still relevant and are needed at present for the present highly technological society. Good traditions should be conserved by different social groups i.e. family, school, organisations, social institutions.

Tradition is one of the Sources of Values. Traditions are one of the sources of values. Various sources of values are religion, philosophy, literature, traditions, science etc.

Religion: Meaning and Importance

Meaning of Religion

Religion is the system of belief in worship of supernatural power of God.

Importance of Religion

Religion is one of the Sources of Values: Religion is one of the sources of values. Traditions, philosophy, literature, science etc. are other sources of values.

Different religions propagate different values. Hindu religion advocates self-realisation or Moksha. Everyone ultimately tries to merge his own self with universal God. Christianity, Islam, Sikhism emphasize a particular way of life based on the doctrines and principles of respective religions. All religions of the world recommend the following common values of life:

1. Simplicity
2. Pursuit of truth
3. Dignity of labour
4. Tolerance
5. Broadmindedness

6. Welfare of mankind
7. Attainment of bliss/Moksha
8. Holy life
9. Purity and simple living.

Religion and Values of Secularism. Religion can inculcate values concerning secularism. Different religious views can be presented through formal, non-formal and informal means of education.

The use of religious stories, biographies, legends, myths, morning prayers, celebration of religious festivals etc. may contribute to inculcation of common values which are within the framework of secularism.

Kothari Commission (1964-66) and Religion. Kothari Commission (1964-66) mentioned: "All religions stress certain fundamental qualities of character, such as honesty and truthfulness, consideration for others, reverence for old age, kindness to animals, compassion for the needy and the suffering."

Varied Views of Psychologists on the Meaning and Importance of Religion

According to Wilson (1978) artifacts have been found indicating that Neanderthals engaged in religious practices 60,000 years ago and since that time humans have produced about 100,000 religions. A few views about religion are given below:

1. Allport's Views on Religion: Religious orientation often characterizes the healthy adult personality. According to Allport there are two forms of religions:

(a) Extrinsic Religion (Unhealthy Religion) is the superficial religion that is participated in for entirely selfish and pragmatic reasons. Such a religion is also called unhealthy religion.

(b) **Intrinsic Religion (Healthy Religion).** Religion that seeks a higher meaning and purpose in life and provides possible answers to the many mysteries that characterize human existence. Such a religion is also called as healthy religion.

Erikson's views on Religion. Religion is something that many people truly need. For centuries, humans have used **religion** to make the events of their lives more understandable and, therefore, less threatening. Without it, according to Erikson, the lives of millions of persons would be filled with uncertainty.

According to Erikson, a key function of religion is to provide a "shared world image. For only a reasonably coherent world provides the faith which is transmitted by the mothers to the infants in a way conducive to the vital strength of hope." In other words, for adults to instil hope in their children, they must have faith in their world. Erikson does not believe, however, that religion is the only thing that can provide a world image conducive to trust, hope and faith. Many people, he says, derive faith from such secular areas as science and social action.

Rollo Reese May's Views on Religion: According to May, true, healthy religion is defined as follows:

"Call it confidence in the universe, trust in God, belief in one's fellow-men or what not, the essence of religion is the belief that something matters presupposition that life has meaning."

According to May, a religious person is one who has found meaning in life, and an atheist is one who cannot, or has not, found it.

May considered religions that required blind acceptance of dogma to be unsound and unhealthy.

Healthy religion allows for creative living that May defines as follows:

"Creative living is that attitude..... which welcomes each day with calm enthusiasm instead of melancholy boredom. It is that state of soul by which one can work with success and satisfaction and occasionally a little joy, can love and move through love into a happy marriage and then enjoy the simple pleasures of a family. The creative person can affirm life in three dimensions - affirm himself, affirm his fellow-men and affirm his destiny. To him life has meaning. He is warmed by the friendship of his fellow and cheered by the confidence that he is of worth to them. Love can be supreme pleasure to him precisely because it is more than pleasure. His work can be satisfying precisely because it is part of a creative purpose larger than any particular work. All of which means that life's fundamental question receives a positive answer: the person has confidence in meaning in his destiny."

Wilson's Views on Religion. According to Wilson and other socio-biologists, "religion is culturally universal, uniquely human, and part of human nature."

Wilson says, "The predisposition to religious belief is the most complex and powerful force in the human mind and in all probability or ineradicable part of human nature."

According to Wilson, religion plays a vital role in allowing humans to live in groups such as tribes or nations. Wilson (1978) says, "Religion is above all the process by which individuals are persuaded to subordinate their immediate self-interest to the interests of the group." Religion does this in several ways but one way is to generate a feeling of kinship among persons who share common beliefs. By holding similar beliefs people, at least symbolically, become related and feeling related, they are more likely to engage in reciprocal altruism. Furthermore, religions almost always sanctify the principles by which believers should conduct themselves. Society depends on reciprocal altruism and religion encourages its practice and creates fear or guilt in those who are inclined to cheat.

Another important function of religion is to simplify life, and religion does this in several ways. In addition to providing believers with a feeling of kinship, religion also encourages the human tendency to divide humans into two categories such as believers and non-believers, members of the in-group and members of the out-group, and friends and enemies.

Social living requires rules and regulations and historically, it has been religion, in one form or another, that has furnished and enforced them. Although it appears necessary that these rules and regulations encourage altruism, give a sense of kinship to members of the community and discourage any practice that is not conducive to survival and reproduction.

Religion typically functions to strengthen and maintain the ethical code by which a society functions, therefore, it is not surprising to find that all of the major religions make strong statements about reciprocal altruism.

Thus religion facilitates societal living in several ways. On the negative side, however, is the fact that religions are seldom tolerant of each other. Wilson (1978) says, "The one form of altrusim that religions seldom display to tolerance of other religions. This is as true for ancient traditions as it is for more modern religions. Each religion is made up of rules, regulations, myths, and ceremonies and rituals. Each religion sanctifies a particular way of social life, provides answer to the great mysteries of life, and makes its adherents believe that they are special in some way, for example, that they are God's favourite people."

Freud's Views on Religion. According to Freud, religion is an illusion and it derives its strength from its readiness to fit in with our instinctual wishful impulses.

According to Freud, our ancestors created a God with the same characteristics as real fathers. When our ancestors were children they turned to their fathers for protection and guidance. Fathers tended to be revered, feared, and relied on. According to Freud, perhaps the uneducated masses will always need the illusions of religion to cause them to restraint their passions but educated, intelligent persons should live their lives according to scientific facts, not illusions. It is time, said Freud, to admit that our ancestors were wrong about religion; miracles never existed; natural disasters kill both believers and non-believers; no life after death occurs; and the course of human history is explained by evolutionary principles rather than the unfolding of a divine plan. Furthermore, although civilization does requires rules, regulations, and inhibitions, these should be justified on rational grounds rather than claiming that they are the will of a deity. In other words, humans should be shown how various sanctions ultimately work to their own self interests and for that reason, should strive to preserve them.

Relationship of Values, Traditions and Religion with Education

Need of Value Oriented Education : Various Views

There is a need of value-oriented education because of the erosion of social, moral, economic, political and cultural values in the present highly technological society. People have become materialistic. A few popular views are stated below:

Indian Education Commission (1964-66). Indian Education Commission writes "The weakening of social and moral values in the younger generation is creating many social and ethical conflicts in Western societies and there is already a desire among some greater Western thinkers to balance the knowledge and skills which science and technology bring with the values and insights associated with ethics and religion at its best.

Challenge of Education. A Policy Perspective mentions the following:

"One of the major crises facing education in India is that of value-orientation. It has been usually argued that the main focus during the last three decades has been on quantitative expansion and consequently adequate attention could not be paid to maintaining standards and quality of education. The output of the educational system is not only of poor quality but degradation of the moral values has also been noticed."

National Policy on Education (1986). "The growing concern over erosion of essential values and an increasing cynicism in society has brought to focus the need for readjustments in the curriculum for the cultivation of social moral values."

"In our culturally plural society, education should foster universal and eternal values, oriented towards the unity and integration of our people.

Such value education should help eliminate obscurantism, religious fanaticism, violence, superstition and fatalism."

"Value education as a profound positive content is based on our heritage, national goals, and universal perceptions. It should lay primary emphasis on this aspect."

Inculcation of Values : Approaches

There are different approaches for inculcating values in others, which are briefly explained below:

Direct and Indirect Approach: Direct approach means teaching values directly to others. Here efforts are made cautiously to teach different values to others. The approach may work for some time but many a time it has its disadvantages. There may be reaction of the learners and sometimes they may give opposite opinions. That will prove rather more dangerous.

Indirect approach of teaching the different values is more convenient and effective. Here teaching is done uncautiously. The learner reads books and is able to catch up values of life here and there. In day to day life situations, he learns values incidentally.

Formal and Informal Approach: When the learners are taught about difficult values by using formal ways, it may not have greater effect. Here materials from books are taught with the motive of teaching certain values. Television is shown by using formal situations in order to inculcate different values. On the other hand, the learner or the receiver of values is unaware of everything. He reads some material from the books and is able to pick up value of life incidentally. This type of learning is of greater value and lasts longer.

Curricular and Co-curricular Approach: According to curricular approach, separate syllabus is framed which aims at teaching different values to the learners. The syllabus is prescribed and teaching is done to finish the syllabus. In the textbooks, the different values may be integrated in different chapters. Thus the students have curricular programme which helps them to learn different values.

According to co-curricular programme, different activities such as singing, poem recitation, drama, debate, declamation contest, essay writing, competitions are organised with the main motive of inculcating different values of life in the youth. There can also be social service activities physical exercises, games and sports. Different activities will help in the inculcation of values.

Ways and means for the Inculcation of Values in Educational Institutions

The authorities in educational institutions can organise various activities and functions for the purpose of inculcation of values in the youth. The head of the institution and the teaching staff can plan and organise a number of programmes for this purpose. A few such programmes are briefly explained below:

1. The textbooks prescribed for the students should contain stories with certain moral lessons. Teachers interested in writing textbooks for the children can help in making the textbooks of this type. Even supplementary readers or books for the children may be written by some teachers in collaboration with others and help in the achievement of the fixed targets.

2. Prizes may be given to the deserving persons for showing honesty, bravery, gallantry, truth, etc. The award of prizes be given to the students in social gathering.

3. Declamation contests may be organized in the institution on themes related to values of life. The contests may be infra-school and then these may be inter-school. Participation in the contests by way of speakers and also by way of audience will have a good deal of impact.

4. National Service Scheme (N.S.S.) need be popularised and its programme of activities be organised vigorously. The students interested in social service at the railway station, at the general bus stand, in the social festivals, in the hospitals, in the villages, in the slum areas be able to do a lot. That way they will pick up those values of life permanently.

5. A few projects for value education may be started in the educational institutions under the guidance of some teachers. The students may start their own canteen with no-profit, no-loss basis. Different groups may control it turn by turn and make its functioning successful. Some students may start a co-operative store where books and stationery on whoelsale rate may be purchased and sold to all the students studying in that school. The basis of the co-operative store should be no-profit, no-loss. It makes the students hardworkers and they will also understand this business and the margin of profit and loss etc.

   In the same way, students co-operative bank, students co-operative post office etc. may be set up in the institution under the guidance of some teacher. All this will inculcate good values of life among the students. Those students will come out as successful social beings.

   Educational institutions should shoulder the responsibility and strive in every possible way for the inculcation of values in the youth. The beginning years in the school are more conducive for it. The teacher will be able to achieve the aims by devoting less time and by paying far less attention as compared to the situation which would be otherwise.

6. Extension lectures based on morality or value-oriented education may be arranged in the institution. Eminent persons specialized in this field may be invited. Listening to the lectures, discussions etc. will help a good deal in this direction.

7. The head of the institution and the teaching personnel should be living examples of values. The institution in itself should be made a centre for moral instructions. It should propagate all types of higher values of life.

8. Book exhibitions on literature related to values be organised in the institution by extending invitations to noted publishers/book-sellers of this area of knowledge. The exhibitions should be thrown open to the students and the community. It will have its effects on one and all.

9. Educational TV can work wonders in this field. Some good teachers can bring out materials related to values in the form of TV serials. Showing such films to the students and the community be made a regular feature of the school.

10. Art and painting exhibitions on themes like moral, social, cultural values etc. be organised in the institutions. Paintings of distinguished artists depicting values be displayed. Such exhibitions will have their effects on the growing personalities of children. Some children might develop their interest in this area of knowledge. On the spot, Art and Painting competitions may be organised on themes related to different types of values. Students of different age groups may be invited from institutions of the region or the state as may be considered proper. Prizes may be given for excellent performances in different age groups. It will highlight the themes of values among the children and through them to the families and the community.

11. Some journal on the theme of values in life may be brought out by an institution. It can be done by some voluntary organisation also. Suitable articles can be invited for publication. The journal may be monthly or quarterly as is possible and its circulation should be popularised. It should be suitably priced so that it is within the reach of majority.

12. Skit, drama competition may be organised in the institution. Assistance may be sought from the District Public Relations Officers. The themes should be values in life- social, moral, cultural, political, educational etc. The different institutions should be encouraged to participate in the competition enthusisasticalty.

13. Value-oriented education should be made compulsory in all the schools. One teacher may be entrusted the duty of assessing the whole teaching of the school in terms of value education. Strenuous efforts should be made to achieve the desired aims with the co-operation of the staff and students.

14. Morning Assembly should be made compulsory in all the educational institutions. It can be of half an hour duration. Apart from morning prayer, good thoughts may be read out by some students and staff members. Religious and national songs may be sung or such poems may be recited.

15. House examinations may be arranged in value education. All students may be asked to qualify it at junior levels say in V standard, VIII standard and also at XII standard. It should be at degree level which may be organised by the university or by the college itself. No student should be considered to have passed the examination without having passed the value education or moral education or the so called religious education.

Traditions, Religion and Education

Traditions and various religions are the two important sources of values. Traditions and religions can be used for inculcation of values through value-oriented education. Following points point out the ways through which traditions and religions can be linked effectively with education in India.:

1. Fundamental principles of ethics are common to all the religions. Gandhiji suggested Wardha Scheme for teaching religious values through education.

2. School assemblies, including morning assembly can foster valuable moral truths.

3. Actual teaching of religious scripture can also be done.

4. Personal influence of teachers can be effective in inculcating religious values and values linked with traditions.

5. Celebration of religious festivals can help in inculcation of desirable religious values.

6. Simple and interesting relgious stores and myths can develop desirable values. The religious stories and myths

can be included in text books related to languages. Teacher can illustrate the values linked with these stories and myths.

7. Teaching of different religions can be a part of syllabus for social studies or history.
8. Extension lectures on traditional values and religious values can be organised under extra-curricular activities.
9. Joint celebrations of religious functions in educational institutions can develop the feelings of respect for all religions.
10. Social service is emphasized in all religions. Social service activities can be organised by institutions on the guidelines of various relgions and traditions.
11. Religious studies can be included in the time-table at various levels of education. Comparative studies on religions, history of religions can be taught.

Central Government Scheme for Strengthening Culture and Values in Education

National Policy on Education (1986) identified promotion of Indian Culture and Values in education as one of the goals of education.

Centrally sponsored scheme of Assistance for strengthening culture and values in Education.

Bodies Eligible for Financial Assistance. Centre sponsors a scheme to assist the programmes that are in line with strengthening of Indian culture and values in education. The assistance is given to the following:-

(a) Government Agencies

(b) Educational Institutions

(c) Panchayati Raj Institutions.

(d) Registered Societies

(e) Public Trusts

(f) Non-profit making Companies.

Components of the Scheme

These are two components of the scheme;

1. Strengthening cultural and value education inputs in the school and non-formal education system.
2. The in-service training of art, craft, music, and dance teachers.

Finance

Budget provisions for this assistance programme are made by the Centre annually e.g. Five Crore for 1999-2000.

Centres for Promotion of Indian Culture

1. Centre for Cultural Resources and Training (CCRT)

Establishment

* It is an autonomous organisation established in May, 1979.
* It is under the administrative control of Department of Culture, Ministry of Tourism and Culture with Headquarter at New Delhi and two regional centres (Udaipur and Hyderabad).

Revitalisation of Education System:

The central goal of CCRT is to revitalise education system by creating understanding and awareness among students about the plurality of the regional cultures of India and integrating this knowledge with education.

Programmes for In-service Teachers:

Organisation of training programmes orientation programmes for in-service teachers from all parts of the country to achieve the following aims:

Development of awareness among students and teachers about problems e.g. environmental problems; conservation and preservation of Indian culture.

Programmes for Foreign Teachers:

Programmes are also organised for foreign students and teachers.

Organisation of workshops, seminars and training programmes for students and teachers.

Various types of workshops, seminars and training programmes are organised e.g. emphasis is given to Indian culture through drama, art, & other ways. A list of the programmes is given below:

Educational tours to monuments, museums, art galleries, craft centres, zoological parks and gardens:

* Camps on conservation of natural and cultural heritage.
* Extension lectures and demonstrations by artists, experts related to arts from schools & colleges.

Collection of Multi-Media

Efforts are being made to collect a variety of mass media on Indian culture and civilisation for use under various programmes of the centre throughout the country.

Scholarships

Scholarships are being awarded to students of age group 10-14 years under cultural talent search scholarship scheme. Students who are studying in schools, are eligible for these scholarships. These scholarship are also considered for those children who belong to such families who are practicing arts and are significant as Indian heritage. Scholarships continue upto 20 years of age or first year of a university degree. 322 students have got scholarships upto 1999-2000.

Teachers Awards

Awards are also given to teachers every year. Each award carries a citation, a plaque, an angavastram and an amount of Rs. 10.000/-.

Zonal Cultural Centres

Aims of Cultural Centres are as follows:

* To project cultural kinships transcending territorial bonds.
* To develop awareness about local cultures.

* To highlight cultural integration irrespective of geographical boundaries.
* To develop national integration through integration of culture & development of awareness.

Seven Cultural Centres

There are seven cultural centres:

1. North Zone Cultural Centre, Patiala.
2. East Zone Cultural Centre, Calcutta.
3. South Zone Cultural Centre, Thanzavur
4. West Zone Cultural Centre, Udaipur
5. North-central Zone Cultural Centre, Allahabad.
6. North-east Zone Cultural Centre, Dimapur.
7. South Central Zone Cultural Centre, Nagpur.

Assignment

1. Define the term "culture". Discuss briefly its material and non-material components.
2. Write varies characteristics of culture. Comment upon the following:

   (a) Views of Indian thinkers on culture.

   (b) Views of Western thinkers on culture.

   (c) Indian culture and its material and non-material components.
3. Discuss the relationship between culture and education. Justify the impact of culture on education. Justify the impact of education on culture.
4. Describe briefly the meaning and importance of values.
5. Explain briefly the meaning and importance of traditions.
6. Discuss the meaning and importance of Religion.
7. Comment upon the types of religion according to Allport.
8. Briefly discuss the views of psychologis s on the meaning and importance of religion.

9. Comment upon the views of Freud on religion.
10. Comment upon the views of Wilson, a socio-biologist and psychologist on religion.
11. "Education and values". Comment.
12. Comment upon need of value-oriented education in India.
13. Discuss briefly the value-oriented education in India.
14. Comment upon traditions, religion and education.
15. Discuss briefly the relationship of values, traditions and religion with education.

11
Social Change and Role of Education

In culture, the material and non-material aspects depend upon the needs of the society. The change occurs in these material and non-material aspects with the passage of time. New challenges are there before every society. New technologies develop for the benefit of mankind. The structure and functions of different social orders change as a result of a number of interrelated and interdependent factors. The present chapter deals with the concept of social change and the factors that influence these social changes in our social orders.

Concept of Social Change

1. Talcott Parsons and others believe in the structural and functional sub-systems of social system. The change in structural and functional sub-systems of social system is the social change.

2. Dawson and Gatis: Cultural change is the social change. Cultural change can be grouped into two categories: material and non-material. Material aspect of culture deals with material of utility while non-material part constitutes habits, ideals, beliefs, attitudes and values.

   State of social development is called as civilization. In the light of above facts, social change means change in material and non-material aspects of society.

3. Johnson: According to Johnson social change may be defined as modification in the ways of doing and thinking of people.

4. Maclver: According to Maclver, change in social structure is called social change

5. Kuppuswamy: According to Kuppuswamy, social change is the change in social behaviour and social structure, norms, roles, cultural values and personality of individuals.

6. V.R. Taneja: According to V.R. Taneja, change in manners, customs, habits, attitudes and purposes is called social change. He is also of the view that open mind and interaction of varied factors (historical, environmental, technological, scientific and so on) brings in social change. There are innovations. An innovation is a new way of looking at things in the light of felt experiences and knowledge, a departure from the old to the new in order to make it relevant to the times. Innovations must be examined, tried and adapted and if found good for society, they must be integrated for the development of society. Regarding types of social change, it is of two types: exogenous and endogenous depending upon the exogenous and endoenous factors bringing about social change. Social change can also be classified as planned change and unplanned change.

7. Gupta: Socio-cultural change can be characterised by three stages (Gupta, 1995): innovation; diffusion; and interpretation. Innovative stage deals with new discovery either in the shape of a machine or an idea. The diffusion stage requires social interactions in which choices or decisions are made by individuals or groups of individuals. The interpretation stage involves the actual adaptation of existing system in order to implement the innovation.

Factors that Influence Social Change

There are many factors (causes) that are responsible for social change. Economic, social, psychological and political factors of social change are briefly described below:

Economic Factors. Economic factors are important for social change. For example, low per capita income of a citizen of a country affects consumption pattern (a social factor), savings (economic factor), investment (economic factor), production (economic factor).

Low per capita income affects other economic factors (low savings, low investment and low production) and social factors (low consumption).

Social Factors: Social factors affect the social change. For example, education, health, housing, social services, food and nutrition, employment are the social factors related to standard of living in a society. These factors affect human resources (non-material component of culture), natural resources (material component of culture), technological resources (material component of culture).

Human resource development depends upon various factors of standard of living e.g. education develops human resource. Better health provisions contribute to his health maintenance. Social services meet the individual's needs. Employment provides economic security. Sufficient per capita income helps an individual in improving consumption pattern, saving and investments.

Human resource development as a result of factors of standard of living also contributes to improve human capital and technological resources. The improvement in resources (human resource, human capital and technological resources) improve economic conditions of the country and the individuals.

Psychological Factors: Psychological factors e.g. personality, intelligence, problem-solving skills, reasoning, creativity, motives, adjustments, needs, physical, social, emotional and moral development of individual, group behaviour etc. affect social change. Fully developed personality of a citizen contributes to social, economic, political, cultural development of a country. Intelligent persons, with well developed reasoning abilities, creativity, contribute to social development. Well adjusted individuals do their best for social development.

Political Factors: Political factors like political system in a country foreign policy, etc. affect social change. For example, democratic political system in India is causing social change in line with parliamentary system of democracy. In America, social change is in progress in Line with Presidential system of democracy. In China, communism is bringing change in Chinese society according to philosophy of communism.

Political philosphies and actions also affect foreign relations, foreign aid which have their own implications on social, economic, and psychological factors.

Political decisions in different countries are different on environmental issues, population regulation, drug abuse, literacy, education, economic decisions, industry etc. Hence social change in a society depends much upon political factors.

Miscellaneous Factors: Geographical factors, environmental factors, population, developmental priorities etc. are other major factors of social change.

Role of Education

Education is a dominant factor which affects the social and cultural behaviours of individuals directly and indirectly. Let's have a brief discussion on the direct and indirect effects of education on socio-cultural changes in context of Indian population. The description on this aspect can be done on the following major headings:

1. Education, standard of living and social change.
2. Education, resources and social change.
3. Education, population situation and social change.
4. Education, environmental problems and social change.
5. Education, existing socio-cultural patterns and social change.

I Standard of Living

Resources.

Population Situation.

Environmental Problems.

Existing Socio-Cultural Pattern.

Education, Standard of Living and Social Change. Factors related to standard of life are education, health, social services, food and nutrition, employment, per capita income and national income, employment, etc. Education is a dominant factor in bringing about change in socio-cultural behaviours of people. Educated members of a society are today developing interest, appreciation, attitudes and values related to factors like health services, employment, per capita income, social services, etc. They are constructively engaging themselves in bringing improvements in these factors and thus trying to improve their standard of living. Education is a single factor which is developing awareness about he contributions of these factors in improving their quality of life. Thus, we can conclude that education is bringing change in the social behaviours of people through the development of awareness of factors of improving the standard of life. Secondly, education is encouraging them to participate in activities related to these factors besides simple awareness. Thus the awareness component as well as developmental component are the functions of education with specific reference to social change in the area of standard of living.

Education, Resources and Social Change: Education affects the development of resources which bring a significant change in the material and non-material aspects of culture of any society.

A few examples are described below:

Education, Human Resource Development and Human Capital Formation: Education contributes to human resource development and tiuman capital formation. Human capital is the sum total of knowledge, skills, initiative, resourcefulness, capacity for sustained work, right interests, attitudes, values, aptitude, and all other human qualities conducive to higher output and accelerated economic growth. The human resource development and human capital constitute components which are the non-material components of culture. Thus education is instrumental in bringing about changes in knowledge, skills, interests, attitudes, values, etc. which are the non-material components of culture.

Education, Technological Resources and Social Change: Technological resources are developing due to new researches and technical education. These resources are being appreciated and utilized by members of the society. People have developed positive attitude for vocational and technical education. Modern values realited to industries based upon current technologies are being internalized by business community. Scientific and technological attitudes and rationality are being given preference today. Thus, education is contributing towards the development of a highly technological society where material and non-material aspects of Indian culture are changing rapidly.

Education, Natural Resources and Social Change: Natural resources like water, forests, petroleum, minerals, etc. are available in plenty in India but we lack adequate knowledge and right attitudes to manage these resources for maximum economic output. Education is providing technical knowledge, and managerial skills. Education is also emphasizing for development of desirable attitudes and values in this regard. For example, through education, desirable attitudes regarding conservation of natural resources. It is only through the development of right attitudes regarding conservation, we will be able to utilize our natural resources for a longer period.

Education, Population Situation and Social Change: Population explosion is a major problem in the national development of under-developed and developing countries. The economic resources are utilized mostly in meeting the basic needs of people and investment in productive activities is less. Investments in developmental plans are to be increased. There is a need to change the opinions and value system of people with specific reference to population problem. Education can be instrumental in the internalisation of right value systems to control this problem.

Education, Environmental Problems and Social Change. Technical advancement and industrialisation are good for us in terms of economic development, but industrial growth and other factors are causing environmental problems which have become a serious threat to the very existence of human race. Educational measures can be adopted to develop awareness among people. Attitudes for healthy environment can be inculcated through education. Thus education is being used today as an instrument to inculcate desirable values related to environmental problems.

Education, Existing Socio-cultural Patterns and Social Change: The existing political systems, cultural systems, social systems and consumption patterns can be analysed and desirable changes can be brought about using education as an instrument. The values of democracy, socialism, secularism, egalitarian, social order, nationalism, modernisation, internationalism, Sanskritisation, Westernisation, etc. can be inculcated through education strategies.

Assignments

1. Discuss varied views on the concept of social change.

2. Comment upon the importance of social change with specific reference to India.
3. Discuss various factors or causes that contribute to social change. Support your answer with suitable examples.
4. Discuss the relationship between education and social change.
5. Comment upon the following:

   (a) Education, standard of living and social change.

   (b) Education, human resources and social change.

   (c) Education, technological resources and social change.
6. "Education is an instrument of social change." Comment.

12

National and Emotional Integration by Education

People's life style is the replica of different social values. As is the society, so are the life styles. There have been variations in life styles from time to time. In an age of autocracy, the life styles become too much limited. In democratic times, when everybody has his own way of life, it is but natural that there will be good many life styles becoming popular. At the time of independence of the country, it was a fully integrated and combined type of society. But with the passage of time, there has been some sort of disintegration. So much so that today it has become a popular trend of life. Perhaps, it is coming out as a fashion of life. Only a few individuals advocate it, but majority of people have their disliking for it. There is disntegration in the personality of an individual. Equally, there is disintegration in the member of a family. It is seen that in a family, different religious beliefs are cropping up. Likings and dislikings also vary from one individual to another in the family. One member of the family wants to have one type of breakfast, another wants a different type and the third one has his own peculiar taste. All this shows a socially disintegrating small unit of a famly. Similar is the case of society, the state and the nation when we review the different aspects of life from various angles.

Disintegration is becoming a trend of life. There is disintegration because of different beliefs, customs, traditions, cultures and values of life. Questions arise - Was it so in the past ? Was it so before the independence of the country ? Was it so at the time of independence of the country ? Perhaps, no. Not at all in that spirit as it is now.

Need of the hour in our country is national unity and integrity. Education can play a very significant role. In the words of Dr. Radhakrishnan, "If India is to remain free, united and democratic, education should train people for unity and not localism, for democracy and not dictatorship."

In the same context, Pt. Jawahar Lal Nehru remarked, "We should not become parochial, narrow-minded, provincial, communal and caste-minded, because we have a great mission to perform. Let us, the citizens of the Republic of India, bring out the integration of the Indian people. We have to build up this great country into a mighty nation, mighty not in the ordinary sense of the word, but mighty in action, mighty in culture and mighty in its peaceful service of humanity."

Nationalism

As per Advanced Learners Dictionary of Current English, nationalism is strong devotion to one's nation; patriotic feelings. It is loyalty, love and devotion towards one's nation. A person who possesses the sentiments and feelings of nationalism is called a nationalist. Mrs. Indira Gandhi said, "Even if I die in the service of nation, I would be proud of it. Every drop of my blood, I am sure, will contribute to the growth of this nation and make it strong and dynamic." So feeling of love towards the country, devotion and spirit of self-sacrifice is nationalism. A true nationalist stands far above party politics and is ever-ready to serve the nation and safeguard it from any type of outer dangers. The fundamentals of national unity are co-existence, tolerance, co-operation and unity.

Definitions

Brubacher says, "Nationalism ordinarily indicates a wider scope of loyalty than patriotism in addition to ties of place. Nationality is evidenced by such other ties as race, language, history, culture and tradition."

According to Humayun Kabir, "Nationalism is that which depends on we-feeling towards the nation."

According to Education Commission Report, (1964-66) "National integration includes a confidence in nation's future, a continuous rise in the standard of living, development of feeling of values and duties, a good and impartial administrative system and mutal understanding."

Dorothy Thompson's view, "National integration is a feeling that binds the citizens of a country."

National Integration Conference Report, 1961. "National integration is a psychological and educational process involving the development of a feeling of unity, solidarity and cohesion in the hearts of people, a sense of common citizenship and a feeling of loyalty to the nation,"

Narrow Meaning of Nationalism

Some people talk of nationalism in the limited sense. They are heard saying-my country and not bothering about others or the country of others. When people limit their views to their own limited sphere, to their own nation only in this age of internationalism, that creates hatred, jealousy, conflicts and that leads to destruction of peace and war.

Hitler's views, Hitler used to say that the Germans have been born to rule over the world and others to be ruled. The concept 'My country flood or bad, should be dear to me' is wrong. This narrow concept destroyed the humanity.

According to Bertrand Russell, "The boys and girls are given the education that their greatest worship or devotion is for that country of which they are citizens and the creed of that worship of the country that whatever the government does is desirable. Therefore, they are taught false History, Political Science and Economics so that they may criticise the lesson of worship of countries of other persons."

Mudaliar Commission says, "There is no more dangerous maxim in the world of today than 'My Country right or wrong.' the whole world is now so intimately interconnected that no nation can or dare live alone and the development of a sense of world citizenship has become just as important as that of national citizenship."

Pt. Jawahar Lat Nehru said, "Nationalism is such a strange element which while it instils life, development, energy and integration, at the same time makes it narrow because on account of it a person thinks about his own country as separate from other countries of the world."

Nationalism and patriotism are not synonymous. Patriotism is old and nationalism and internationalism are modern. Brubacher rightly remarks, "Nationalism ordinarily indicates a wider scope of loyalty than patriotism."

Broader Meaning of Nationalism

True or pure nationalism means love and devotion for one's country but not at the cost of hatred for others. A true nationalist is a well wisher of everyone and he strongly believes in world peace. In fact, the spirit of true nationalism in a person tends to make him a lover of internationalism.

Prevailing Situations

It becomes an important study to find out the real causes of the present fast deteriorating social situations. There is more and more of disintegration with the advent of life. The following seem to be the causes:

Frustration

In the society we find that there is too much of frustration seen almost in everybody. Nobody seems to be satisfied with his lot. Of course, the degree of frustration varies from person to person, and from family to family. The businessman has his own frustration, the employee has his own, the teacher has his own frustration, the Head of an institution has his own, the teachers and the students have their own reasons of frustrations. Whatever may be the cause of frustration but all this makes them lovers of loneliness and seclusion. They dislike sharing their views with others and they find it difficult to have belief in others.

Corruption

The corruption in society is rampant. We may take up any circle, social, political, economic, there is favouritism and disfavouritism. Justice to one and all is rather disappearing. Corruption from the top to the lower levels is spreading various type of ills in the society. Naturally it has its disintegrating effect on the growing and developing personalities of the children.

Loss of Good Leadership

The society of today has no shortage of leaders but surely there is dearth of good leaders. A good leader is replete with truth, honesty, goodness and sincerity. Such a person is a true leader, is the true path shower but the society of today is devoid of any such leadership. The educational institutions are generally headed by the most unfit type of leaders. Many teachers don't possess the qualities of leadership and they fail to imbibe such qualities among the students under their control. In political circles also, there are no good leaders. These so-called leaders come to the people at the time of elections only and then they are never seen before the next elections. They are only the mongers of votes who come for their own selfish motives only. In the capacity of political leaders in a circle or a region whatever is expected out of them, they fail to do any such thing. They even fail to hold the reins of the country truly. Whatever they do and whatever they stand for, their own selfish interests are involved. In the society, the real leaders, social workers etc., who are ever ready to serve others in times of difficulty, are also very much limited. Day by day their number is decreasing.

Public Clashes

Public life mostly stands disturbed. Every now and then, various types of communal clashes are seen. Whenever such clashes are noticed, they present a very gloomy picture of the whole society. The commonness of such incidents in the present day life is having an increasing effect on the students community. Whatever happened in the social circles is now very often seen in the centres of learning. Groups of students are seen fighting leading to confusion and chaos.

Lack of Patriotism

Patriotic feelings showing the oneness of the people for the country are fading. People are becoming more and more selfish and their thoughts and ideas are mostly of self-centred type. Perhaps they have forgotten the sacrifices made by the great heroes of the country for the glory of the nation.

Need and Importance

The greatest need of the country is to strengthen itself through national unity. National unity is essential for any country at any time. It is doubly so for India in view of varied compositions of her population, the vast distance that separates her different parts, the vastly varying climate and physical feautres that condition the daily fives and occupations of the people and above all, because of the period of rapid change-social, political, economic and technological -through which she is passing to discover her bearings in the modern world. We should have full faith in nationalism and national understanding. Varied views on need and importance are given below:

Pt. Nehru gave a call to Indian people saying: "The time has surely come when every Indian must look within and ask for himself whether he is with the nation or with a particular group. This is the challenge of our time that every man, woman and child must face."

Kothari Commission: According to the Kotharl Education Commission Report, national understanding (national integration) implies:

1. A confidence in the nation's future.
2. A continuous rise in the standard of living for the masses which included reduction in unemployment.
3. A deep sense of values and obligations of citizenship and growing identification of the people, not with national loyalties but with nation as a whole.
4. Assurance of good and impartial administration, equal treatment for every citizen.
5. Mutual understanding and respect for the culture, tradition, and ways of life among different sections of the people. Only a united nation can stand firmly like pillars to shoulder without any type of outer or inner threats to its existence. The present situations that prevail all around further necessitate to have a strong united nation. Then and then only it will be able to exist prosperously in the teeth of any type of oppositions or threats. The following points show clearly that national integration is the only way out to overcome the different type of deteriorations going on in the country:

A Democratic Country

At the time of independence, the national leaders accepted the country as a democratic republic. Now that has to be maintained. For this, proper education about the democratic values has to be imparted to all the citizens of the country.

Misunderstandings of any type in the understanding of the democracy will have to be ended.

A Secular Country

India accepted secularism though there exist people who have faith in different type of religions. Everybody has his firm convictions in his own religion. It is the process of education which helps them understand that the basis of all religions is the same and the ultimate goals are also the same. Only the way of life which is actually very temporary, is different. Thus people will be enabled to have full faith in secularism. Naturally then, they will have all regards for each and every religion.

Unity in Diversity

In India there are people of different cultures. In many cases, it is seen that there are too many variations among the different cultures. In the absence of conscious efforts uniting them, they will remain separated and will not perhaps share their living together with others. So some type of inter-cultural ties have to be thought of and implemented.

Geographical Variations

India is a vast country which is spreading far and wide. If we see to the geographical placement of different religions, the South and the North are the two extremes with lot of divergences and variations. People of one region have different ways of life, traditions, conventions which "have hardly any similarity with the ones being maintained in the other region. There is need of making them understand that they are Indian nationals. Their progress and prosperity depend upon their beliefs in true national values.

Variation of Languages

Different people living in India use different languages for their communication purposes. There is so much of difference that one can hardly be understood properly by the other. It is rather difficult to give equal recognition and status to all the languages. A useful way out has been arrived at through the process of education. The three language formula surely helps in this regard when everybody accepts Hindi as the national language and learns it. It unifies all the people of the country to some extent. Then,

English as an international language further strengthens the contacts of the people with one another. The importance of mother tongue remains becaue it is given the status of first language.

Dr. Radhakrishinan. It the words of Dr. Radhakrishnan, "If India is to remain free, united and democratic, education should train people for unity and not localism, for democracy and not dictatorship."

Pt. Jawahar Lal Nehru beautifully remarked, "We should not become parochial, narrow-minded, provincial, communal and caste-minded, because we have a great mission to perform. Let us, the citizens of the Republic of India, bring about the integration of Indian people. We have to build up this great country into a mighty nation, mighty not in the ordinary sense of the word, but mighty in action, mighty,in culture and mighty in its peaceful service of humantiy."

National Integration Through Emotional Integration

National integration is not a mechanical process, it is rather a psychological process. In fact, emotional integration is the basis of national integration. Emotional attachment links people and persons firmly and strongly.

Humayun Kabir's view, "National integration does not depend on race or language or religion or geography, singly or collectively, though they help, but on the feeling of belonging to one nation."

Pandit Nehru's view: "Let us, the citizens of the Republic of India stand up with straight backs and look up at the skies, keeping our feet firmly planted on the ground and bring about the synthesis, the integration of the Indian people. Political integration has already taken place, but what I am after is something deeper than that, an emotional integration of the Indian people so that we may be welded into one strong national unit, maintaining at the same time all our wonderful diversity."

National Integration: Efforts at the National Level

Following steps have been taken at the national level to foster national integration:

1. Formation of National Integration committee under the Chairmanship of Smt. Indira Gandhi.

2. Appointment of Emotional Integration in Committee under the Chairmanship of Dr. Sampurnanand.
3. Periodical Conference of Chief Ministers to discuss the problem of national integration.
4. Establishment of National Integration Council.
5. Conference of the Vice-Chancellors to tackle the problem of national integration.
6. Setting up of an organising committee by the standing committee of National Integration Council to conduct organised campaign against communication in the country at a massive scale, with which all the political parties, eminent sociologists and educationists would be associated and so on.

Role of Education in National Integration

Education plays an important role in bringing about national integration. Ever since India's independence, many efforts have been made in this direction. There have been commendable achievements, but much more need to be done. Let us visualise the efforts and the achievements.

Achievements

1. A national system of education (10+2+3) has been accepted almost in every state of the country. Earlier there were different systems of education in different states. It is a very favourable step in the direction of national integration.
2. The same system of education implies the same curriculum. The textbooks prescribed for different school classes have been nationalised. Now NCERT syllabus or CBSE syllabus is prescribed. All school text-books have been published by NCERT. Those books have been adopted or adapted in different states of the country.
3. Language problem has also been solved to a great extent. Three language formula has been accepted. Regional languages, mother tongue, national language of the country and international languages have been accepted. This is another step in the direction of national integration.

4. Efforts have been made to have the same pay scales for the employees all over the country. It has successfully been done in the case of college and university lecturers. More efforts are being made to have same pay scales for other cateogries of employees all over the country.

Thus we find that something has always been done at various levels in the interest of national integration. Education can still play a more crucial role in the attainment of objectives leading to national integration.

The Kothari Commission Report observed that one of the basic objectives of education should be to accelerate the process of social and national integration.

The Gajendra Gadkar Committee of the National Integration Council observed that education from primary to postgraduate stage should be reorented to:

1. serve the purpose of creating a sense of Indianness, untiy and solidarity;
2. inculcate faith in the postulation of democracy and
3. help the nation to create a modern society out of the traditional one.

The latest in this regard are the observations made in the National Policy on Education 1986. While indicating the essence and role of education, it states:

"Education has an accelerating role. It refines sensitiveness and perceptions that contribute to national cohesion, a scientific temper and independence of mind and spirit thus furthering the goals of socialism, secularism and democracy enshrined in our Constitution."

Ways and Means

Here below are suggested some ways and means:

Promotion of national integration must be an important aspect of school curriculum at different stages. The whole school climate should be conducive for inculcating different values related to national integration. Lectures or sermonisations do not help much. The teacher himself should be a living symbol of national integration. A really good teacher is able to effect the students in desired ways.

Dr. Radhakrishnan remarked, "National integration cannot be built by bricks and mortar. It cannot be built by chisel or hammer. It has to grow silently in the minds and hearts of men. The only process is the process of education.'

Specific Role of the Teacher

1. The teacher of language should talk about not only the languages that he is teaching but also some other languages in his teaching, he can draw comparisons with other languages. His knowledge of other languages will imbibe in the learners love and regard for different languages.
2. In the teaching of History, the teacher can draw the attention of the students to the achievements of mankind. They learn how to appreciate the works and deeds of bravery of others. The history of India's struggle for freedom reminds the students about the sacrifices made by others. They will learn many things and value their hard earned freedom.
3. Through teaching Civics, the teacher can explain the rights and duties of the citizen. The students will be able to understand the Constitution. The topics such as fundamental rights, duties, system of government, etc. emphasize the unity of the government.
4. In Geography, the teacher explains to the students about the location of different regions, raw materials produced in there and thus their use in the factories which are located there or somewhere else. The teaching of this subject thus highlights the interdependence of various regions and areas. The policy of give and take between different regions helps in bringing the people together.
5. Through the study of Science, the students become logical and rational. They tend to have a scientific temperament. Generally, people quarrel over trifles or other petty issues which don't have any scientific basis. When the students are able to think logically, they are then not prejudiced just for nothing. Thus, the study of Science helps in inculcating the ideals of national integration.

Head of the Institution and His Team of Teachers

The Head of the institution and his team of teachers can plan many things for national integration. These can be put to practice to achieve the goal of national integration. Here below are explained some ways and means:

1. The head of the institution and his whole staff should present a unique example of united whole.

   The Head should ensure that there is one team of the whole staff and not a team divided into groups. It will stand reflected fomally or informally. It will have its effects on the student community.

2. The schools should celebrate days which are of national importance. Instead of declaring a holiday, the school should celebrate the Republic Day, Teachers Day Childrens Day. It will have a very good effect on the minds of the young learners.

3. Festivals of different communities from which the students come may be organised. The celebration of one festival may be for one house which may have students from different communities. This will increase mutual understanding and also add to national integration.

4. Respect and love for national flag, national anthem, patriotic songs, etc. should be maintained. The students should be encouraged to recall such songs.

5. Intra-school and inter-school essay writing competitions, declamation contests on themes related to national integration may be organised from time to time. Prizes may be given to the students having outstanding performances.

6. Extension lectures by persons of eminence who worked for the nation, may be arranged. The students will be able to learn many things from their experiences of life. They should be asked to confine their speeches to the themes of national integration or emotional integration.

7. Inter-state matches for different games, inter-state youth festivals for different cultural items may be organised. It will increase mutual understanding among students of

different cultures and social groups. It will naturally help in national integration.

8. Tours and trips to different places may be organised with the sole educational purpose of better mutual understanding. It will improve upon feelings of unity.

National integration is the need of the hour in the present day social set-up of life. Education is the main instrument which can help in achieving the desired goal. There is need of using education in its right perspectives. In the words of National Integration Committee, "Education should, therefore, be re-oriented and made more broad based. It should aim at:

1. Equipping students with intimate knowledge of the different aspects of this country including the events that had led to the freedom.
2. Encouraging all studies and activities which lead to greater understanding between communities and states, thus fostering a feeling that the country and its sources leading to the citizen who thereby acquires certain rights and privileges alongwith corresponding duties and responsibilties."

According to National Integration Committee, "Reading material provided to boys and girls in schools and colleges should be properly examined. Text-book Committee should receive definite guidance in this particular matter. If possible, model books should be prepared by the centre. There are some Dont's which can be kept in mind while preparing textbooks. The Centre should appoint a Committee for this purpose. Popular books on regional Indian heroes known for their national outlook should be prepared."

Assignments

1. What do you mean by national integration ? How should educational places and programmes be geared to the task of national integration ?
2. Why is national integration important for us ? How far can we achieve it through education ?
3. 'National integration without emotional integration is a myth.' Explain and give illustration.

4. As a headmaster of high school what programmes would you start in your school for propagating national integration ?
5. What is national integration ? How does it differ from emotional integration ? How can education promote both ?
6. 'Education should be for nationalism'. Suggest ways and means for making it all successful.